BOOKS

BY

WILLIAM
GREIDER

SECRETS OF THE TEMPLE:
HOW THE FEDERAL RESERVE RUNS THE COUNTRY

THE EDUCATION OF DAVID STOCKMAN
AND OTHER AMERICANS

THE TROUBLE WITH MONEY

BY WILLIAM GREIDER

469-490

WHITTLE DIRECT BOOKS

Photography by George Lange with the following exceptions: Gerald Corrigan by
Andrew Popper/Picture Group, page 5; Vladimir Lenin, The Bettmann Archive, page 13;
Hugh McColl by Mitchell Kearney, page 18; Bo McAllister provided by
the San Antonio Savings Association, page 27.

Illustration by Jeffrey Smith, page 3; Bush Hollyhead, page 11; Terry Widener,
page 36; Walt Gunthardt, page 50; David Shannon, page 53; Bush Hollyhead, page 74;
Steve Carver, page 92.

Charts by Genigraphics Corporation

Library of Congress Catalog Card Number: 89-05171
Greider, William
The Trouble With Money
ISBN 0-9624745-0-9
ISSN 1046-364X

The Larger Agenda Series

The Larger Agenda Series presents original short books by distinguished authors on subjects of importance to managers and policymakers in business and the public sector.

The series is edited and published by Whittle Communications L.P., an independent publishing company. A new book will appear approximately every other month. The series will reflect a broad spectrum of responsible opinions. In each book the opinions expressed are those of the author, not the publisher or the advertiser.

I welcome your comments on this unique endeavor.

William S. Rukeyser
Editor in Chief

CONTENTS

6:52 AM, San Juan, Puerto Rico. A loaded plane arrives.

Federal Express serves more than
118 countries on six continents.

It was a delicious moment in the history of America. The country's citizens were entitled to feel expansive about themselves, for events in the late 1980s formed a message of national vindication. Almost daily, the headlines from Europe and Asia described the unraveling of dictatorial regimes and the triumph of popular will over rigid, centralized power. Commentators declared that the Cold War was over and we had won. Elected political leaders could be forgiven for flourishes of patriotic self-congratulation. Communism, it turned out, was a dying ideology. It was Lenin, with his melodramatic pronouncements about "moribund capitalism," who was headed for the dustbin of history.

In Washington, this sense of national triumph made all other matters seem small and transitory. The Republic faced the usual assortment of problems and controversies, and the elected representatives quarreled, as always, over the remedies. But the reigning spirit of the day was self-satisfaction.

In many respects, the conservative political order that Ronald Reagan had brought to Washington seemed fulfilled. Communism was exhausted and retreating abroad. At home, the new conservative majority on the Supreme Court was dismantling important tenets of liberalism. If America's modest welfare state had not been decimated during eight years of Reagan, it was at least stymied in its growth. The long-running Reagan prosperity, though its benefits were unevenly distributed, continued to churn forward smartly with low unemployment, generating a sense of contentment. The regulatory controls by which Washington governed private economic affairs were now pruned back significantly, and there was no political will to reverse that trend.

With President Reagan in mellow retirement, his inheritor occupied the White House and enjoyed spectacular popularity ratings in his opening season as Chief Executive. George Bush toured Poland and Hungary and celebrated their liberation. In the Oval Office, he settled comfortably into his chosen role as the manager of continuity, proposing to fix this and that, but mainly to keep the conservative status quo on track. Even the Democratic opposition in Congress succumbed to the mood, and with lowered voices its leaders began to negotiate amiably with the new Republican leader in the White House.

How *normal* it all seemed, as though the great ideological battles that had roiled during the Reagan years were now all settled, or at least willed away. Fred Barnes of *The New Republic* spoke for the current conventional wisdom when he announced the dawning of a "new era [of]...consensus, conciliation, and compromise, a lot like the 1950s and early 1960s, and just as trivial and boring."

The deficit problem—the debate over national priorities that had consumed political energies for so long—virtually disappeared from the front pages (though not, of course, from the federal budget). The Bush administration and the Democratic leaders of Congress agreed that since public contention had failed to end their stalemate, they might find mutual massaging in private more productive. Nothing had changed except that periodically the principals emerged to compliment one another on their improved relationships. Rumors of "progress" regularly swirled through the capital.

Meanwhile, the Federal Reserve, true to its own institutional reflexes, was attempting to stabilize prices in the only way it knew how: by suppressing the economy. The Fed is an obscure center of governing power, poorly understood by most citizens. But nearly everyone grasped that the central bank's stern management had been at least as instrumental in reshaping the American economy during the 1980s as had Reagan's economic policies. The Fed had first eradicated double-digit inflation by engineering a long and painful recession, then preserved its victory by restraining and modulating economic growth throughout the long-lived Reagan recovery.

> **H**ow *normal* it all seemed, as though the great ideological battles that had roiled during the Reagan years were now all settled, or at least willed away.

In measured steps, during 1988 and early 1989, the central bank had raised interest rates, effectively increasing the price of credit in the United States by roughly 35 percent (see chart, page 10). The Fed then backed off a bit, as the domestic economy responded in predictable ways to this gradual punishment. Housing and homebuilding industries went into decline, followed by the automobile industry and retailing. Eventually, steel, paper, and chemical production, along with most other kinds of manufacturing, went into general retreat. These developments were the classic steps that normally led to recession whenever the Federal Reserve imposed sustained tight money policies on the economy, but this time the ominous news

The financial-market traders on Wall Street, who had badgered the Federal Reserve to arrest inflation, reassured the political community that no one would be hurt as a consequence.

failed to dim the aura of good feeling, at least in Washington.

The financial-market traders and analysts on Wall Street, who had badgered the Federal Reserve to brake the economy and arrest inflation, reassured the political community. No one would be hurt as a consequence, they said. A recession was "not in the cards," as one analyst put it, because this time the Fed did not intend to provoke one. Instead, Wall Street's consensus held that the economy would experience a therapeutic "soft landing" in which growth would moderate and inflation would subside, but the general suffering of a genuine contraction would be avoided.

As industrial production fell and unemployment began to rise, some nervous analysts revised their estimates and conceded that the wished-for soft landing scenario might entail a "mild recession." Still, they insisted, nothing worse than that. The leaders of the Federal Reserve were widely praised for their skillful manipulation of the vast economy.

In Congress, the only significant legislation enacted was the reform and reconstitution of the troubled savings and loan industry, an unfortunate casualty in the Eighties prosperity. This refinancing of the federally insured deposits in hundreds of failed thrift institutions was unpleasant business, and it was embarrassing because the bailout would inevitably cost the taxpayers hundreds of billions of dollars. Still, the legislators proceeded with admirable bipartisan cooperation, promising to clean up the mess for good. The ingenious politicians had found a way to commit upward of $160 billion in public money to rescue the S&Ls—with only marginal impact on the reported budget deficit.

The problems in the savings and loan industry, it was widely explained, could be attributed to entrepreneurial excess—mainly the extravagant behavior of certain Texas freebooters whose S&Ls were insufficiently supervised by federal regulators. The new legislation would close down or refinance the hopelessly insolvent firms and prevent similar episodes in the future by imposing stern new rules on the survivors. Never again, the Congress and the president promised.

Politicians in Washington wished to believe all of this, and they hoped that voters would believe it too. Because the official debate was so narrow and evasive, it resembled a conspiracy of wishful thinking, a tacit agreement between both political parties, among liberals and conservatives alike, not to puncture the aura of normalcy. As long as visible events did not dramatically contradict them, the governors would presume that all was for the best.

One can almost imagine the ghost of Lenin, somewhere in the netherworld, smiling fiendishly as he takes note of certain objective realities in the American condition, unpleasant facts that political leaders have declined to face. Capitalism has certainly not been overthrown as he predicted, but Lenin might argue that the American system has advanced nicely down the road he suggested—toward pathological contradiction and decay.

T he most striking symptom of disorder was reflected in the core of the American economy—the financial system—which was caught up in a perpetual frenzy of activity. Sober leaders of finance worried especially about what they saw unfolding. E. Gerald Corrigan, president of the Federal Reserve Bank of New York, expressed his anxieties in the cautious language preferred by conservative central bankers: "While it is beyond debate that the process of change and innovation has brought with it important benefits," Corrigan wrote, "there persists a nagging sense of unease...that is prevalent among financial-market practitioners themselves—that all is not well. To some extent, that sense of unease seems to grow out of the concern that legitimate broad-based public-interest considerations about the structure and stability of financial markets and institutions are being swept aside in a helter-skelter of events that lacks an underlying sense of direction and may be weakening the system."

To E. Gerald Corrigan, president of the Federal Reserve Bank of New York, the pace of change in the financial markets was of "a revolutionary character."

Among other things, Corrigan worried about the hyped-up financial system—the ability to trade faster and faster thanks to computer technology and the government's deregulation of banking and finance. The financial markets were trading stocks and bonds and other credit instruments in furiously expanding volumes. They had also invented a bewildering stream of new and exotic financial instruments for the players. "A virtual explosion in financial transactions" is how the president of the New York Fed described it—a pace of change that was of "a revolutionary character."

The New York Fed itself, for instance, served in 1986 as a clearinghouse for a daily flow of financial transactions exceeding $1 trillion, and Corrigan estimated that another half-trillion or so in deals was cleared elsewhere. Roughly speaking, that meant that *each day* Wall Street was buying and selling and swapping pieces of financial paper with a presumed value equal to one-third of the U.S. gross national product.

To what end? At what risk? Daily trading volume on Wall Street multiplied thirtyfold in a decade, not including the swollen transactions of foreign exchange, according to another worried observer, Albert M. Wojnilower, a senior adviser and former chief economist at First Boston Corporation. This fury of trading, Wojnilower noted, "can hardly be essential to the efficient allocation of the country's resources."

During 1984, First Boston, one of the world's leading bond houses, itself transacted deals totaling $4.1 trillion—exceeding the nation's GNP. The average holding period of long-term treasury bonds used to be measured in years; in the mid-1980s, it shrank to about 20 days. The market in interest-rate swaps, an esoteric investment that hardly existed at the beginning of the decade, then exceeded $150 billion in outstanding volume.

In free-market theory, all of this was the logical, predictable, and desirable outcome of withdrawing government controls from the financial system. Federal regulation added, at least marginally, to the cost of doing financial transactions, and deregulation would naturally reduce the cost. Once something is made cheaper, people can be expected to buy more of it. The political struggle to deregulate the

Albert M. Wojnilower, former chief economist at First Boston Corporation: The fury of trading on Wall Street "can hardly be essential to the efficient allocation of the country's resources."

financial system and cast off the New Deal legal restraints was driven partly by the new technologies of computers and telecommunications, but more specifically the campaign was fueled by the competitive rivalries among the different financial sectors themselves. The old regulatory rules were too rigid to adapt to the changing markets, and inventive financiers found ways around them or lobbied for outright repeal. When the government's credit-control system was overwhelmed in 1980 by double-digit inflation, Congress capitulated, and most of the old legal strictures on lending were abolished.

Free at last from loathsome regulation, the financial markets and allied banks responded by producing a lot more paper. In this case, the "product" that was liberated was the distribution of money and credit—a social contract as well as a private commodity and an economic link. Social trust, stable commerce, and dynamic capitalism all depend on the reliability of this product. The consequences of fraud and folly in this instance are profound, not at all comparable to the failure of an auto company or a steel mill. What worried sober observers was the risk, as Corrigan put it, that the public interest was being "swept aside in a helter-skelter of events."

Wojnilower observed that "the combination of technological advance and deregulation has given free rein to the ingrained human propensities to borrow, lend, speculate, and gamble too much.... The reason there is so much trading is that people enjoy trading. For many, it has a narcotic attraction. As with gambling, we enjoy trading particularly when the price of admission is low, there are many winners, and some of the prizes are prodigious."

Captains of American industry, among others, felt the consequences quite directly in their own lives. Corporate executives had always been obliged to treat their bankers respectfully and to court the good opinions of stock-market analysts, but now the largest companies became captive to finance in new and destabilizing ways. On one front, managers felt the hot breath of financial adventurers who could assemble staggeringly large packages of debt, buy out the shareholders at a generous price, and profitably cannibalize the corporation. On another front, the fortunes of U.S. export industries now rose and fell capriciously, not based on the quality of their own performance but on the money traders who gambled on currencies in foreign-exchange markets. The international trading of currencies has always been a function of commerce between nations, but now the trading of goods across national boundaries accounted for only about 5 to 10 percent of the swollen volume in money trading. Real goods produced by real manufacturers became the tail wagged this way and that by a large, distant dog—the mood swings of financiers and bankers around the globe.

The liberation of lenders from government regulation also meant, of course, the liberation of borrowers. They were now free to pay whatever the market decided was the correct price for credit. The terms of bank lending and other forms of credit had been closely regulated by the federal government since the New Deal—especially the legal ceilings set on the interest rates that lending institutions could charge. In part, the interest-rate limits reflected the biblical admonition against usury, the sinful exploitation of desperate borrowers by powerful holders of wealth. More directly, the interest-rate controls were an implicit subsidy for the borrowers, both businesses and consumers, justified by the liberal Keynesian premise that easy credit was integral to stimulating vigorous economic growth. The interest-rate ceilings, less obviously, also served as an important lever by which the Federal Reserve controlled the pace of the overall economy.

In the 1980s, for the first time in 50 years, the U.S. economy went through the cycles of recession and recovery free of the arbitrary inhibitions on lending that Washington had so long imposed. Credit would be treated, in a sense, as a private transaction between consenting adults; usury was decriminalized, not unlike gambling and certain once-forbidden forms of sexual behavior.

Usury was decriminalized, not unlike gambling and certain once-forbidden forms of sexual behavior.

Now the marketplace would set the price of money and presumably determine what was a prudent risk and what was not. Instead, as Wojnilower once put it, a new form of Gresham's law came into play, "in which profligacy drives out prudence."

The results are now prominent in the pathological symptoms of excess that make people nervous about the future. First, the domestic economy—consumers, businesses, and the government—borrowed at the highest levels since World War II, raising debt to troublesome proportions. Second, the mountain of debt accumulated in this decade was contracted under the most unfavorable of terms; borrowers paid the highest real interest rates of the 20th century.

One did not need an economics degree to grasp the portent of these facts—a vast array of borrowers were overleveraged, paying extraordinary interest rates. If unfavorable economic conditions threatened to depress their incomes or profits, even temporarily, their balance sheets would be squeezed, and as they fell behind on interest payments, they might be forced to default on their loans. Of

1:29 AM, Memphis, Tennessee. Fleet ready for loading at main hub.

Federal Express owns the largest
all-cargo air fleet in the world.

course, if enough borrowers went under, so would their bankers.

Actually, throughout the Eighties this process of debt liquidation was already under way; the spectacle of bankrupt borrowers and failed financial institutions unfolded during the 1980s on a scale Americans had not experienced since the Great Depression. For several years, this distress had been moving around the country in rolling waves of debt default, from agriculture and oil to real estate and housing. Each episode produced severe regional crises but failed to excite national alarm. In every case, the debacles were blamed on the excessive greed of the victims themselves—farmers in the Midwest or real estate developers in Texas. The disorders were said to be temporary. The system was absolved. The waves of default did not go away, however, but merely moved to new sectors and different regions. The "nonperforming loans" that blighted the bank balance sheets did not decline but continued at unprecedented levels, given the long recovery cycle.

Denial of the problems became increasingly difficult because the system of deregulated banking and finance did not—as the free-market theory had so often promised—impose much discipline on itself or its customers. The competitive combat for market shares, encouraged by deregulation, also drove financial institutions of every kind to assume greater risks, just as an overcrowded market forces other kinds of businesses to lower their standards. Bankers were supposed to be the sober scolds who imposed restraint on borrowers' reckless ambitions, but, as Wojnilower caustically observed,

INTEREST RATES 1988-89

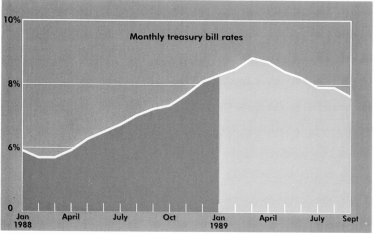

SOURCE: FEDERAL RESERVE SYSTEM

bankers too were caught up in the values of the Me Generation.

And with good reason. Unlike other kinds of business, banking has a safety net underneath it—explicit and implicit guarantees from the federal government that, in grave circumstances, it will come to the rescue. When the banking industry lobbied Congress to be freed of federal regulatory controls, it did not ask to be liberated from the benefits of federal protection—deposit insurance, bargain-rate liquidity loans, and other forms of support provided by the Federal Reserve. None of these was removed. On the contrary, the federal guarantees to banking and finance were vastly expanded during the 1980s, covering financial activities not even mentioned in law and extending far beyond what the public imagines. American taxpayers are unwitting cosigners on the mountain of debt that the economy has accumulated.

The federal government has provided a safety net under banking, guaranteeing that it will come to the rescue in grave circumstances.

The conservative era, in other words, has created a bizarre version of laissez-faire—a half-pregnant system that liberates banking and finance for new adventures in risk-taking, yet assures the players that if something goes terribly wrong and they sustain great losses, the U.S. government will step in and pick up the tab. This offends principle and has produced recurring disorder and crisis.

The process of picking up the tab is under way—and on an awesome scale. The 1989 legislative rescue of the savings and loan industry dwarfed anything that had occurred during the economic wreckage of the 1930s. But then so did the spectacular federal rescues of the major commercial banks that failed. The size of these government interventions was unprecedented in U.S. history or, for that matter, in the history of banking anywhere. The costs grew larger in part because regulators and politicians of both parties wishfully deferred the day of accounting for as long as they could.

The bastardized system would produce more losses of a similar nature, given the unnatural separation of risk and responsibility that had been built into federal law. What frightened some financial experts was the knowledge that given the wrong set of events, the S&L and bank bailouts could be dwarfed by the other potential liabilities facing the national treasury. Thanks to the expanded safety net that regulators had provided private finance, the public was implicitly obligated to clean up the wreckage that might result from private risk-taking across a staggering range of credit functions—from the mortgage-backed securities market to junk bonds.

The claims on taxpayers' money were only part of the problem, however. The other unsettling dimension was the very different role that the federal government had assumed—that of the major force in the private realm of banking and finance. Inevitably, the process of massive defaults and financial rescues had drawn the federal government deeper and deeper into the private marketplace, producing political interventions that were the precise opposite of what conservative theory had promised. Washington did not get off the backs of bankers; it simply joined them in banking.

The federal government was now an important owner and manager of financial institutions and, given its girth, an influential arbiter of market shares—picking winners and losers, assisting in the consolidation of financial power, providing capital to certain ambitious players, and dooming others to extinction. All told, the feds would wind up acquiring about one-fifth of the savings and loan industry, perhaps much more if things went badly. The government was the principal shareholder of the second-largest bank in Illinois and of the largest bank in Texas. It was the silent partner in scores of other banks and financial institutions. It had become a real estate magnate on a gargantuan scale, owning hundreds of billions in marketable assets, from farms to shopping centers.

Conventional wisdom held that these facts, like other pathological symptoms, were aberrations, embarrassing but temporary anomalies that reflected transient "adjustments." Other financial experts, who understood the underlying dynamics of how this system worked, were not so sanguine. They had watched the federal presence grow and grow throughout the 1980s, despite the conservative rhetoric then in fashion, and they saw nothing to reverse that trend as long as the political community declined to act.

Genie D. Short, the vice-president of the Federal Reserve Bank of Dallas, studied the compromised condition of free-market banking and the forces that were driving the federal government toward deeper and deeper involvement. She reached a gloomy conclusion. "Those policies raise serious questions about the long-term viability of a private financial system in this country," Short wrote in a 1989 essay. She later added, "If we continue the way we are...we are going to wind up with a nationalized financial system. The way we are trying to resolve current problems is already a form of nationalization—government-owned operations."

While Marxist regimes struggle to adapt their command economies to the free market, the citadel of democratic capitalism seems to be stumbling toward a de facto system of nationalized finance. The development, if it continues unimpeded, will constitute the ultimate nightmare for conscientious conservatives—an era of reform that was launched by their faith in laissez-faire economics and that ends perversely with the politicians in control of private finance.

Lenin, on the other hand, would be delighted by the irony. He always said that in the last decadent stages of capitalism, the road to true socialism would start at the banks.

The era of conservative hegemony has produced grotesque contradictions for laissez-faire conservatives, but big-government liberals are also deeply implicated. After years of contention, most Democrats supported financial deregulation or even championed various measures. Fundamentally, the present mess is the result of combining the old liberal mechanisms for federal stewardship with the permissiveness espoused by the free-market theorists. Neither camp is prepared to acknowledge its own role in what they created together.

The argument is not ultimately about ideology, but about the real consequences for real people and real enterprises in the American economy. The pathological symptoms of excess could indeed evoke some sort of calamitous break in the financial system, an event that would destroy innocents alongside the guilty. Moreover, these contradictions are already extracting enormous costs by sapping economic energy, distorting business decisions, and aggravating social inequities. A financial system has been created that thwarts future prosperity instead of fostering it.

Vladimir Lenin always said that the road to true socialism would start at the banks.

Ten years ago, the staple arguments for deregulation always invoked the international economy, claiming that the U.S. must abandon political controls over domestic finance in order to compete aggressively in the global marketplace. Today, paradoxically, the case might be reversed: unless the United States reregulates, by imposing broad public goals and values on the behavior of private banking and finance, the nation won't regain its footing in the international economy. The realm of finance sets priorities for the nation, and in the present arrangement, its priorities are warped, focused on short-term gain and speculative credit on a vast scale.

If politicians find it hard to admit error, so do influential bankers, professors of economics, and editorial writers. The governing elites, elected and unelected, are unwilling to face these pathological symptoms forthrightly, partly because to do so would require them to admit grave flaws in much of what they have espoused and sold to the general public during the last two decades. Too much energy and commitment was devoted to this cause; too many reputations are at stake.

Many of these opinion leaders, furthermore, do not themselves lose by clinging to the status quo; they prosper enormously. Underneath the dense technicalities of finance, there are always, inescapably, class arguments about who shall be favored—the borrowers or the lenders, the ambitious entrepreneurs who need low-cost capital for their ventures or the cautious owners of wealth who must lend it. These daunting political choices become another reason the politicians wish to avoid the question.

Given the natural inertia of politics, it is far more convenient to muddle through, patching up the system as each crisis arises, propping up its torn parts and hoping that somehow or other these "adjustments" will eventually work themselves out. That, in essence, is the government's strategy, supported by both political parties and widely endorsed by private authorities.

America has stumbled onto very dangerous ground. The fissures that are now so visible will not go away on their own because they are caused by deep contradictions in the money system itself. As I explore various elements of that system, I hope to persuade the open-minded that only fundamental reform—a reregulation of the financial system—can work the nation out of these contradictions.

The core conflict involves both the weakened regulatory rules that now govern finance and the Federal Reserve's management of the economy through monetary policy. These interact with a third realm, international finance, and set off destabilizing waves that sweep across the economy at large, claiming hapless victims. In different parts of America, the economic consequences are already well understood, though perhaps the solutions are not. Farmers understand that the system is malfunctioning, and so do some important manufacturing executives and Texas bankers. After the stock-market crash of 1987, even many on Wall Street began to wonder. In Washington, the subject is not on the agenda.

A mordant historical question is implicit here: Does the American political order have the capacity to act in a timely fashion—that is, before some sort of bloody economic crisis demolishes the status quo? Or is that too much to expect of a polity governed by comfortable elites, leading an electorate ignorant about finance? To act now, before ruinous consequences shatter the status quo, requires a substantial body of thinking citizens willing to reexamine the old shibboleths with clear eyes and to hold them up against the new realities. Given the smugness of this era, no one can be sanguine about how the question will be answered.

Only fundamental reform—the reregulation of finance—can work the nation out of the contradictions in the money system.

4:37 PM, Somewhere in the American West. Courier making pick-ups.

Federal Express couriers make more than
350,000 daily delivery stops in the U.S. every day.

9:41 AM, Somewhere in the Far East. Courier making deliveries.

With more than 14,000 couriers outside the U.S.,
Federal Express expertly serves a growing economy.

PLAYING WITH HOUSE MONEY

CHAPTER 2

Hugh L. McColl, the chairman of NCNB Corporation of Charlotte, North Carolina, was not known as a diffident banker. He liked to talk about NCNB in the most ambitious terms, and his boastful tone occasionally rankled more conservative competitors who thought of him as something of a gunslinger. His bank was started in 1960 as the North Carolina National Bank, with a piddling $480 million in assets. By the 1980s it was the fastest-growing "super regional" in the Southeast. Through aggressively acquiring other banks in Florida and the Carolinas, NCNB had increased its assets to $29 billion.

McColl held a still grander vision of what might yet be accomplished. In April of 1988, addressing his hometown college audience, he suggested that someday NCNB would be big enough to compete head-on with the money-center banks of Wall Street—the huge multinational institutions descended from Morgan and Rockefeller.

"I find it interesting, purely on an intellectual level," McColl mused, "to consider that the very term *money-center bank* may be in the process of becoming an anachronism." The term traditionally referred to the nine largest American banks, most of them within walking distance of one another in lower Manhattan. But modern telecommunications had practically obliterated the geographical boundaries of banking. As one of McColl's aides put it, the telephone lines run to Charlotte as well as to London and New York, and so do the high-speed computerized systems that can

Hugh L. McColl led NCNB Corporation overnight from the 18th- to eighth-largest among U.S. banks—a coup that ranks as one of the greatest management strokes in the history of American banking.

now link everyone everywhere to the global financial markets.

"You could have a financial institution that meets every historic definition of a money-center bank located anywhere in the country," McColl contended. "You could even, for example, have this sort of institution headquartered someplace like Charlotte, North Carolina."

Three months later, McColl's boastful conjecture came true—literally overnight. On the last weekend in July of 1988, NCNB doubled in size. It jumped from 18th to eighth on the list of U.S.

commercial banks and suddenly grew from $29 billion in assets to $60 billion. The little bank from North Carolina that had grown up so fast was now indeed within the prestigious inner circle of American banking powers.

Surely his coup ranks as one of the greatest management strokes in the history of American banking. The story of NCNB's extraordinary growth has a democratic flavor that appeals to almost everyone—an American fable of free enterprise in which small-town guys with true grit demonstrate that they can out-hustle the big boys from the city. When Hugh McColl tells the NCNB story, he makes banking sound positively romantic.

There is only one thing wrong with the fable: the bankers from Charlotte, in addition to their true grit, had a powerful fairy godmother in Washington on their side. The agent that made Hugh McColl's dream come true overnight was the federal government. It awarded him the largest banking franchise in Texas on terms so favorable that, once Wall Street analysts understood the deal, the price of NCNB's stock doubled.

NCNB may well become known as the money-center bank that Uncle Sam created. Among scores of others, NCNB's case is the most spectacular example of how, in the era of deregulation, the federal government has become the all-powerful intervener in the financial marketplace. The government awards huge market shares at bargain prices to those it considers worthy and dooms thousands of other financial enterprises to punishing disadvantage. Given the way the money system now works, the federal government does not have much choice but to wade deeper and deeper into the realm of private finance, as owner, silent partner, and fabulous dealmaker.

The deal, in this instance, was NCNB's acquisition of First Republic Bank Corporation of Dallas, which failed like most of the other major banks in Texas because of hemorrhaging loan losses from oil and real estate. The collapse of oil prices two years earlier had been widely hailed as a bonanza for the American economy, the ultimate victory in the Federal Reserve's stern campaign against price inflation during the 1980s. Stocks and bonds rallied furiously with the news. The collateral consequences and public costs were not mentioned at the time, but they ultimately outweighed the gains. The Texas economy crashed, wiping out borrowers and bankers even more drastically than had the rolling recessions that swept through agriculture and manufacturing in the Midwest.

The federal government is still cleaning up the mess in Texas and will be doing so for at least another decade to come. Federal regulators have so far pledged $8.2 billion for the cleanup of seven major bank holding companies in the state and another $30 billion for the rescue of failed savings and loan firms. As almost everyone now grasps, this is just the beginning of the cost to American taxpayers.

NCNB acquired control of $20 billion in bank assets with a mere $210 million in up-front money. The Federal Deposit Insurance Corporation (FDIC), which took control of the insolvent bank, could have closed down First Republic, liquidated its assets, and paid in full all of the insured depositors—people and businesses with accounts up to $100,000. The FDIC chose instead, as it always did with the largest bank failures in the 1980s, to keep the bank going no matter what the cost, prop it up with a huge infusion of new capital, and find a buyer who would agree to make it viable again.

First Republic, the regulators decided, was another celebrated bank that was "too big to fail." To keep it alive, the feds estimated that they would spend $4 billion to swallow the bank's loans. They had no real option but to guarantee *all* depositors, not just the mom-and-pop accounts. Otherwise, the multimillion-dollar investors who had bought First Republic's CDs would have fled en masse, a modern bank run executed by wire. In that event, no amount of federal intervention could have helped.

The peculiar doctrine of "too big to fail" is another contradictory legacy of the conservative order that ruled during the 1980s. It violates both the free-market principle and the common sense of fairness. It has profound implications for future arrangements of power within the U.S. economy. Nevertheless, the government has decided de facto that certain banking enterprises, the largest in the land, will be kept operating no matter how tattered their condition or culpable their managers. The Federal Reserve and other regulators, in those cases, will extend a blanket guarantee to all depositors in the threatened banks, not just to those with deposits of $100,000 or less, who are covered by federal deposit insurance. In some instances, the government will also guarantee other creditors who have lent to the bank, perhaps even bondholders in the bank holding company.

This is new law, in effect, though it has never been enacted by Congress or even seriously debated. When the reality of federal banking supervision first surfaced in 1984 with the rescue of Continental Illinois Corporation, regulators grudgingly acknowledged to angry congressional inquiries that yes, it was true: the largest dozen or so banks would not be allowed to close their doors under any circumstances, whatever it might cost the government. After the financial debacle in Texas, in which regulators rescued seven of the state's largest banking chains, it became clear that "too big to fail" protects a much larger list of institutions—at least the top 50 or 100 banks in the country.

Why would federal regulators make such a leap without explicit congressional authorization? Because the alternative, they feared, would be a general calamity in the banking system. If one large bank went down, wiping out billions in uninsured deposits from other banks, pension funds, local governments, and foreign investors, the failure would provide more than "market discipline"; it would induce market terror. What former Federal Reserve chairman Paul Volcker and others feared was that, once burned, these large depositors would become anxious about money-center banks that had similar troubles. The result might be a rippling circle of casualties at the very top of the American banking system.

When Continental Illinois, then the eighth-largest bank in the nation, foundered in the spring of 1984, Chicago depositors weren't the ones who brought it down. Institutional money managers from around the world, including other banks, did. When they belatedly got wind of Continental's deeply troubled loan portfolio, they began pulling out by wire, dumping Continental's large-denomination CDs instantly and by the billions of dollars. It was the modern equivalent of a bank run.

Continental, like almost all of the largest banks, depended on the money market to fund its operations; every day it borrowed approximately $8 billion from investors around the world. When they panicked, Continental hemorrhaged. Within 48 hours, it seemed doomed—until the feds came to the rescue. The near-failure reflected a new form of vulnerability in the banking system, one that grew directly out of the modernization of finance, the interlocking nature of high-speed transmission, the huge flow of transient money, as well as the hubris of bankers.

In other times, perhaps the Washington regulators would have accepted the collapse of a major bank as a message of caution to other bankers and investors. In the extraordinary turbulence of the 1980s, though, this did not seem to them a tolerable risk. Virtually every one of the largest U.S. banks was overexposed in its third-world lending. Some had dangerously large portfolios of failing loans in oil, real estate, and other sectors. If the collapse of Continental set off a panicky flight of big investors seeking safe haven for their billions, where would it stop? "In my judgment," said William Isaac, then

Regulators feared that failure of any of the largest banks would provide more than "market discipline." It would induce market terror.

chairman of the FDIC, "we would have had worldwide chaos."

To prevent that, the government offered its assurances and pumped billions into the bank to keep it afloat. The government became the owner of the bank, effectively nationalizing it, although Washington didn't call it that. Five years later, Continental Illinois, now named Continental Bank Corporation, was healthier (and smaller), but the feds still owned nearly 26 percent of it.

The case was not an aberration, as many supposed. The doctrine born in extreme circumstances endured as the rule because extreme circumstances also endured.

NCNB's deal with the federal government vividly embodied the new doctrine. On the surface, entering Texas banking did not seem like a smart move, but McColl and his associates knew better. They had negotiated for four months with FDIC chairman William Seidman and had won remarkable protection from loss. Four or five other large banks had serious bids on the table and argued strenuously for them, but the FDIC found that McColl's would be least expensive to the agency. The federal insurance fund would put up 80 percent of the capital and give NCNB an option to buy it out over the next five years at a bargain price—105 percent of book value—if the Carolina bankers did well in Texas. They were almost sure to do so, even if Texas remained depressed, because the FDIC will take virtually all of the bad loans off First Republic's books and absorb the cost of liquidating them. Once it became manager, NCNB could dump an unlimited number of other First Republic loans onto the FDIC if the loans looked like losers.

The arrangement created a rare institution: a Texas bank that didn't have anything but good loans on its books. Even well-run conservative banks and savings and loans that had successfully managed their way through the debacle of the Eighties were still struggling with badly blighted loan portfolios. Now they would be up against the largest bank in the state—one that no longer shared such a handicap.

"We think there's going to be a tremendous winnowing of banks in Texas," Frank Gentry, director of corporate strategy and planning at NCNB, said, "because everyone out there who has not gone through the same window we did is crippled."

NCNB could hardly lose. While the federal government was assuming responsibility for the billions of dollars of First Republic's bad loans, it was also granting NCNB the right to carry over those bad loans as a tax write-down on its own future earnings. Thus, according to Gentry's estimate, the new bank in Texas was worth between $1 billion and $1.3 billion to NCNB in real money—bottom-line tax savings—regardless of how it performed in the troubled Texas economy.

"NCNB got the tax deal of the millennium," a Dallas tax attorney said with evident admiration. Rauscher Pierce Refsnes Inc., an investment banking and brokerage firm, summarized the transaction: "NCNB blitzed its competitors....The FDIC was mesmerized with the potential of the joint venture. To participate in the transaction, the FDIC accepted all of the risk, advanced 80 percent of the capital requirements, and limited most of its return through the bargain option price. As a result, the FDIC gifted $450+ million of value to the shareholders of NCNB."

"An acrobat ends up making a trapeze act look easy," explained Gentry. "People are now saying the First Republic deal was easy. But, in point of fact, we went to see the FDIC in the first weekend in April, and we stayed on their doorstep until they decided this thing. For anyone who thinks that was an extraordinarily good deal, my question is, why didn't they think of it?"

The tax break was something else. It stirred enough political heat that the Internal Revenue Service subsequently indicated that the next time it wouldn't give the same concession. But the tax shelter was a crucial ingredient in securing the FDIC's approval because it off-loaded a billion dollars or more of the deal's cost onto the Treasury in the form of lost taxes, thereby effectively reducing the cost for the FDIC, which is funded by bank-industry premiums. In this instance, NCNB apparently was simply smarter about the possibilities than were its rivals. The Charlotte bank got a favorable ruling from the IRS, then showed the arithmetic to FDIC chairman William Seidman. It was a good deal for both of them, and Seidman took it.

"The law required that the FDIC take the least costly bid for the FDIC," Gentry explained. "It did *not* say 'least costly to the federal government.'"

Thus, every participant followed the rules to his satisfaction, if not to the taxpayers' benefit. The federal regulators were amazingly generous in the negotiations, though that does not suggest any sort of political influence. If political cronyism was pushing the bank regulators to do stupid things about Texas banks, that undoubtedly occurred in December of 1986, when the Federal Reserve and the Office of the Comptroller approved the merger of Dallas's two largest banks, Republic Bank Corporation and Interfirst Corporation, to form First Republic, the bank that became NCNB's when it went under. Neither of those federal agencies has ever adequately explained why it supposed that the merger of two large failing banks would create one strong one.

The First Republic bailout was not, after all, much different from many other bailout transactions; it was only larger. Once the feds had decided to negotiate to buy a piece of a failed institution, they inevitably looked like chumps in the bargain, holding almost all of the risk and letting someone else pick up the opportunity on the cheap. Rescues of other Texas banks that were too big to fail followed similar outlines.

A flurry of expensive savings and loan deals, executed after the presidential campaign in 1988 by the now defunct Federal Home Loan Bank Board, elicited similar complaints, for the FHLBB also provided outrageous tax benefits to those entrepreneurs willing to accept the carcasses. Investor Ronald Perelman put up $315 million for an S&L with $12 billion in assets and was awarded almost $900 million in tax benefits. The law in these matters has become flexible—terms are negotiable, case by case. Danny Wall, the former chairman of the FHLBB and the director of the recently created Office of Thrift Supervision, was criticized for negotiating so many dubious patch-up deals, but he responded that neither Congress nor the president was prepared to confront the problems squarely until after the election. "They gave us a Band-Aid and said 'take care of it until 1989,'" Wall said. "That's what we did."

Special benefits to NCNB were only beginning to accrue in the summer of 1988. Initially, Wall Street analysts were skeptical of NCNB's judgment; then McColl and his associates briefed them on the profitable inner dynamics of the acquisition. They emphasized, for instance, that earnings per share would increase almost immediately for NCNB stockholders, regardless of what happened to the Texas economy or First Republic's business. Once convinced, the market drove the stock higher—from $22 to $46 a share in 12 months—and that gave Hugh McColl the ability to raise lots of new capital for other acquisitions. Indeed, NCNB bought out the FDIC's ownership far ahead of schedule, albeit at the bargain price.

"I don't think the federal government did us any favor on purpose," Gentry said. "We got a wonderful deal, but we made the best offer. I'm not going to apologize for that. But it is true that because we got a good deal, our stock went up, and that gives us the ability to make acquisitions."

3:52 PM, Minneapolis, Minnesota. Message relayed.

With Federal Express' advanced satellite-based communication system, the status of your package is just a phone call away.

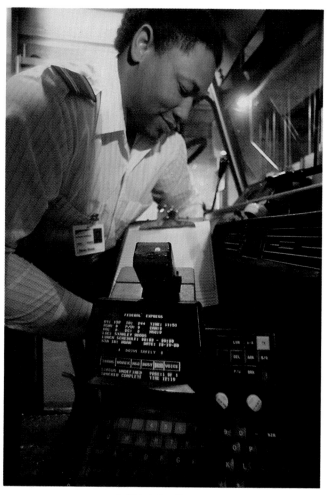

3:53 PM, Eau Claire, Wisconsin. Message confirmed.

DADS,℠ our digitally assisted, in-truck computer terminal,
alerts Federal Express couriers within seconds of your pickup request.

The first foray was aimed at a southeastern rival and Georgia's largest bank, Citizens and Southern of Atlanta, an acquisition that would have hopscotched NCNB up to sixth-largest bank in the nation. McColl styled the $2.4 billion proposal as friendly, but the C&S managers and directors did not see it that way. When they resolved to fight the takeover, NCNB cheerfully withdrew, confident that other mergers lay ahead.

Various senators in Washington were unsettled by all of this, especially when their local bankers called to complain that they might be swallowed by a well-heeled shark that was financed by federal regulators. NCNB executives shrugged off the complaints. They were—and are—unbashful about their intentions: to form an aggressive bank that expects to grow by making more large acquisitions in the future. "If we ever merged with New York [money-center banks]," Gentry surmised, with NCNB's characteristic sense of reserve, "I don't think it would be because some money-center bank acquired us. It would be the other way around."

"The most obnoxious thing going on in Texas," W. W. "Bo" McAllister, chairman of San Antonio Savings Association, declared, "is NCNB Corporation." The newly dubbed NCNB Texas National Bank "is the most predatory pricer in the state—they don't care what they pay for funds," McAllister complained to *The Wall Street Journal* in the spring of 1989. Since Texas National was willing to pay higher interest rates on its CDs, other, weaker institutions were forced to match them or lose the deposit funding necessary to do business. NCNB Texas National had a powerful silent partner—the federal government. In a sense, the bank was playing with "house money."

Bo McAllister, chairman of San Antonio Savings Association: "The most obnoxious thing going on in Texas is NCNB Corporation."

McAllister was not exactly a free agent himself. His own S&L had been placed under the control of federal regulators; it was one of the so-called zombie thrifts that were the living dead of finance. In 33 states the federal government was essentially operating 261 savings and loans that were broke, keeping them going until Congress sent the billions needed to arrange more mergers or buyouts.

Shortly after entering the Texas market, NCNB rankled local sensibilities by advertising five-year CDs that would pay 15 percent interest for the first 90 days. Texas banks complained that the Carolinians were bending the rules and asked the state bank commissioner to investigate. Texas Commerce Bankshares Inc. of Houston ran newspaper ads flaunting photos of its "native" Texan managers (neglecting to mention that when loan losses multiplied in

1986, Texas Commerce had been acquired by Chemical Bank of New York). NCNB officials pointed out that they were just trying to serve the consumer market, and besides, profitable operations would reduce the eventual cost to the federal government.

"The idea that we shouldn't play to win—" Gentry said, "I don't know how to deal with that."

Charles T. Doyle, the CEO of Gulf National Bank in Texas City and a board member of the Independent Bankers Association of America, had brought his chain of five community banks "through all this hell in glorious fashion," and he resented the federal presence that was now distorting the Texas market. "If you talk to NCNB's top management, they'll probably tell you they made money on those promotions advertising rates that were out of the market range," Doyle said. "Well, that's probably true. Because the government took out all their bad loans and guaranteed margins on their portfolio. If you took...all of the loans out of my portfolio that I don't make money on, then I could afford to pay a better rate than the other bank down the street, too."

In fact, there was a bit of Texas chauvinism in the complaints aimed at NCNB; the problem was much broader than one bank or even one state. When Texas suffered its worst economic distress, the money market began demanding a "Texas premium"—slightly higher interest rates on CDs from Texas financial institutions. While investors may have guessed that the feds would come to the rescue

TROUBLED SAVINGS AND LOANS

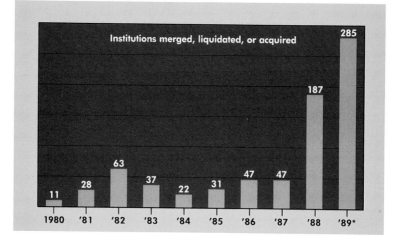

Institutions merged, liquidated, or acquired

1980	'81	'82	'83	'84	'85	'86	'87	'88	'89*
11	28	63	37	22	31	47	47	187	285

and protect their deposits, they demanded a more profitable return as extra insurance, anyway. Now that the federal government was present as the major owner of Texas' failed institutions, the Texas premium had returned, stimulated by the very S&Ls and banks that were in government hands.

In addition, the FDIC had begun running its own "hot money" desk, selling jumbo CDs in the money markets and channeling the funds to the zombies in its stewardship. An FDIC spokesman defended the practice as necessary to keep the zombies funded until they could be sold or restructured. Critics called it the Phoenix program, a droll reference to the anti-insurgency campaign of the same name in Vietnam. The idea that these failed institutions would spring back to life seemed to them as wishful as the U.S. war strategy in Indochina.

In the meantime, however, the loss of deposits from customers lured away by federally subsidized banks was directly absorbed by the healthy institutions that had been soberly managed—particularly the smaller, solvent banks like Doyle's. These had no expectation of federal subsidy but had to compete in the money market against the scores of thrifts and banks that were now under the protective federal wing and had nothing to lose.

Paying inflated rates to raise deposit funds was, in fact, the heart of the problem in the first place. It was made possible by the bastardized form of financial deregulation in the 1980s. When the legal ceilings were taken off interest rates, the federal insurance coverage was simultaneously increased. Banks and S&Ls were encouraged to take excessive risks in the era of deregulation because they were assured that the federal government would pick up the pieces if they failed. Shareholders, supposedly the disciplinary force in finance, went along for the ride, seeking the highest return. They usually did not bail out and dump their stocks until the eleventh hour, when it became clear that the financial institution was failing. Once banks and S&Ls were in trouble, they had no incentive to pull back and behave more prudently. On the contrary, with nothing to lose, they proceeded to take even greater risks, practically all underwritten by U.S. taxpayers.

"Before, they were screaming about stupid management at these institutions," Doyle complained. "Now we've got them kicked out, and the government's got it, and they're doing the same thing— paying 75 to 100 basis points [0.75 to one percentage point] more on CDs and, in some cases, advertising that they are stronger than ever. Yet these banks are nationalized! That really infuriates us bankers."

Playing with house money is a legitimate concern, an FDIC spokesman conceded, but not one that federal regulators can avoid in the present circumstances. The law says that regulators should resolve these matters with the least cost to the insurance fund, and the cheapest solution seems to be propping up the losers instead of liquidating them and paying off only insured depositors. "From a public-policy standpoint, it's a very difficult issue to grapple with," the spokesman agreed. "I'm not saying the critics are simply crying sour grapes."

One stark fact in particular drives the Texas bank wars. Texas has too many banks. Given the new economic realities of $18-per-barrel oil, almost everyone grasps that several hundred of the state's 1,500 banks are going to go under or be merged out of existence. In some ways, Texas is a microcosm of the nation. America has about 14,000 commercial banks, and given the economic forces driving the financial system toward greater and greater concentration, in coming years thousands of banks are likely to disappear or lose their independence.

Charles T. Doyle, the CEO of Gulf National Bank in Texas City, says that federal government backing of large banks threatens to push smaller banks like his out of business.

Regardless of whether this trend is irreversible or in the public's long-term interest, the most troubling reality is this: The federal government is actively driving the consolidation process by encouraging smaller, weaker players to fold their hands and by promoting certain others to stronger positions in the contest. "All this does, when the federal government is making deals like NCNB or propping up others, is to put the banks who are on the margin into the pit," Doyle said. "They're pushing them into the ditch."

The era of conservative reform has put the federal government directly into the role of determining market shares for the distant future and punishing those who resist the trend of consolidation. This role is informal but potent—economic tampering that resembles the dramatic market interventions of the New Deal era and that mocks the laissez-faire bromides of Reagan conservatives. Although no one wishes to say so explicitly, the concentration of financial power appears to be the federal objective. This is true at least at the major regulatory agencies: the FDIC, the Federal Reserve, and the Office of the Comptroller. They are the agents who must supervise the many thousands of institutions and who have recently done such a poor job of it.

The feds are, in effect, picking the winners. Under certain conditions, a federal presence in these outcomes could be justified as rational economic planning in the public interest, if the choices were made according to broad principles that were both equitable and directed at goals that most people shared. But no one has been invited to discuss the choices. The conservative administrators are playing an improvised game of patch-up, seizing the best bid that might reduce the turmoil. The financial system is obligated to serve the nation's needs and is failing to do so now, despite the public subsidy and protection. The hope that a few irregular deals will lead to a stable order has again and again been disappointed.

Big is beautiful, in the eyes of federal bank regulators. Public policy clearly penalizes smaller banks and provides rewards—a much greater safety net and implicit subsidy—to the largest institutions. In Texas, for instance, Doyle sees indifference by federal regulators toward the smaller community banks, even the healthiest ones. "They don't want to deal with players like us," he said. "They only want to deal with players in the billion-dollar class who will buy all of the banks and branches. It's a hell of a lot easier for them to deal with a few big banks—banks that are too big to fail."

The image of the Texas hustler is picturesque: the reckless banker in cowboy boots who built fancy glass office buildings and went bust when he couldn't fill them. For politicians and policymakers, it is comforting to believe that Texas high rollers are the problem. Then the governing elites can tell themselves that once the Texas bloodshed is cleaned up, the banking system will return to the stable, reliable conditions that once prevailed.

Unfortunately, the evidence does not support the wishful thinking. The Texas gamblers, it is true, were more outrageous (and more costly) than bankers anywhere else in the nation, but then Texas and other oil states went through more dramatic economic plunges than did other regions. They bet wrong on the future of oil and real estate, but thousands of other bankers, large and small, who were operating in much less threatening environments, also made awful mistakes. After Texas, the worst jurisdiction in the country in terms of amassing billions in savings and loan losses was Orange County, California, the seedbed of Reagan conservatism and a place that enjoyed extraordinary prosperity.

Blaming Texas alone is a dangerous illusion because it obscures the steady and alarming deterioration elsewhere. After six years of steadily rising bank failures, unmatched since the 1930s, the U.S. banking system still had 1,406 "problem banks" in 1988, according to FDIC examiners. That was nearly 11 percent of all commercial banks. It was more than double the number of banks that were in trouble in 1983, when everyone was coming out of a deep recession. The number of "problem banks" subsided somewhat in 1989, down to about 1,270, partly because several hundred of the "problems" had been merged or liquidated.

The region most recently afflicted with troubled banks, according to *The Wall Street Journal*, was New England, one of the most prosperous in the nation during the 1980s. Its overconfident bankers were awash in bad real estate loans. All over the country, beyond the obvious casualties, U.S. banks in general continue to carry an ominously high level of nonperforming loans—a problem that normally abates as an economic growth cycle continues. This time, through the long Reagan recovery, the bank problems have grown right along with the economy.

If everyone everywhere seems to be committing the same errors, that ought to suggest that something in the system itself—not just the sins of individual bankers—is encouraging foolishness and irresponsibility. A good many experts, in both academia and business, agree that this is so. Most blame the federal government: the illogical way it enforces bank regulation, in particular, and the unprecedented level of interest rates imposed by the Federal Reserve through the 1980s. The high real rates sap the balance sheets of borrowers and produce waves of defaults that engulf the banks.

True-blue conservatives have a simple solution: roll the clock back to before 1933, when federal deposit insurance was created, and let bankers and their customers relearn the invigorating lessons of a genuinely free market. In other words, reintroduce the discipline of bank runs, the occasional storms of panic that would wipe out hundreds of banks (and with them the savings of innocent depositors) and that would paralyze the economy in the process. Though this approach is popular at conferences of conservative economists, it is not a solution that politics or banking is ever likely to embrace.

Others propose a modified version of the same idea. Restore discipline to bank lending, they say, by making the bank stockholders and depositors share more of the potential loss. John Reed, chairman of Citicorp, recommends, for instance, an insurance system that covers only 85 percent of deposit losses in the event of a bank failure. Others want to scale back federal insurance to a ceiling of $40,000 deposits (it was raised to $100,000 with financial deregulation in 1980), and let everyone above that ceiling experience the consequences of parking their money in the wrong bank.

These and other variations might work to instill an improved measure of responsibility among bank managers. They would certainly induce a greater degree of nervousness among bank depositors, especially the ones who buy large-denomination CDs. The money market in large CDs used to provide a form of marketplace discipline on banks as investors demanded higher rates from suspect institutions. But that leverage has dissipated in the permissive Eighties. The buyers of million-dollar CDs know that their money is safe regardless of reckless bankers—as long as they park their wealth in an institution large enough to guarantee that the feds won't allow it to fail.

But the doctrine of "too big to fail," not the terms prescribed for federal deposit insurance, is the heart of the matter. Unless the federal government rethinks "too big to fail" and its broader implications for society, nothing significant is going to be altered. In fact, if the government changed the rules on deposit insurance without facing the other issue, it would simply drive the large-scale depositors to the biggest banks in the country, where they know their money would be safe. John Reed of Citicorp or the officials of NCNB can endorse without qualm the idea of cutting back deposit insurance because they know that *their* banks are too big to be affected. In the unlikely event that Citicorp or NCNB got into terminal difficulty, their large depositors would be unharmed. The depositors know that and so do the bankers.

Ultimately, the only way out of this dilemma is general reform and reregulation across a broad front. That will require profound changes in the way the public and the government regard the financial system and its proper role in the economy. Meanwhile, the people in charge will keep making deals, patching things up, and hoping for the best, while the public, innocently unaware, assumes ominous new levels of obligation for the gambles undertaken by private bankers.

Reform will require profound changes in the way the public and the government regard the financial system and its role in the economy.

10:05 AM, Portland, Oregon.
The Powership 2™ system speaks directly to our main computers in Memphis.

In use at more than 7000 customer automation sites,
the Federal Express Powership system streamlines the shipping process.

THE FUNERAL HOME

CHAPTER 3

Given the momentous nature of what Congress and the president had accomplished, the event received insufficient fanfare. In the summer of 1989, by legislative act, Washington created a new corporation that is destined to become the largest real estate company in the world. By its nature, it will also be a gargantuan financial institution, the largest in America and perhaps second in the world only to Japan's postal savings system. The company will make billion-dollar real estate deals across the nation in the name of the U.S. government, which owns it. Nothing quite like it has been invented in Washington since the darkest days of the 1930s, when Franklin Roosevelt created alphabet agencies to counteract the Great Depression.

This creature dwarfs anything spawned by the New Deal. It bears an innocuous official name—the Resolution Trust Corporation, or the RTC. The banking and real estate lobbyists who shepherded the idea through Congress refer to it more aptly as "the funeral home." The Resolution Trust Corporation is where all of the "bodies" are stored—hundreds of thousands of them—that constitute the collected real assets from the most spectacular financial debacle of the 1980s: the failed savings and loan industry.

The rough working estimate is that, as federal regulators dispose of the insolvent lending institutions, the RTC will acquire real assets valued at as much as $400 billion. If things go badly in the economy, if the bailout legislation was premised on overly optimistic assumptions (as it almost certainly was), then the funeral home may wind up with much, much more in its storehouse of disposables. In addition to its current assets, it will eventually contain even more raw land, shopping centers, tens of thousands of private homes, skyscraper office buildings, factories and businesses, apartment buildings, resort condominiums, trailer parks, and on and on.

Naturally, with money like that on the table, firms of every kind are swarming to do business with the RTC, buying and selling and swapping the carcasses. This new government agency will doubtless contract out a lot of work to private dealers, for it would take an army of federal bureaucrats to manage all of those properties. From its infancy, in fact, the RTC has been trapped in a major political dilemma. If it disposes of its vast holdings too rapidly, it will depress market prices for competing dealers and developers. Why build or buy a new office building when the feds are selling theirs on the cheap? The political pressures to avoid this competitive damage by the government are already quite apparent, and as Congress created the funeral home, it warned the officers not to dump bodies on already depressed real estate markets. Yet if the RTC does not promptly dispose of its assets, even at fire-sale prices, then it will not raise the additional billions needed to continue the closing of other failed S&Ls. If the liquidators run out of funds, they will have to come back to Congress and ask for even more money for this fiasco. The politicians don't wish to be faced with that either.

The "funeral home," or the Resolution Trust Corporation, is where all the "bodies" are stored: the assets of the failed savings and loan institutions.

As staggering as these facts are, the government's embarrassing surplus of real estate takes on an even more melancholy meaning when it is laid alongside another social reality: the national crisis in housing and home ownership. Both of these catastrophes can be blamed in large measure on the same government policies—the recklessness and financial chaos made possible by deregulation.

The dislocations in housing evoke images of despair not seen in America since the Great Depression. Every city, as well as most small towns in the nation, is now familiar with the forlorn tableau of homeless people huddled in doorways, sleeping in boxes or on heating grates, shuffling between church basements and parks and public shelters, often with small children in tow.

But the housing crisis is not just about the homeless people who are so embarrassingly visible. It is also about the less obvious loss for the American middle class—the inability of young families of moderate means to afford their own homes. During the 1980s, for the first time in four decades, the proportion of the population that owned homes declined steadily nearly every year, in almost every age group. Most of the decline was absorbed by one group—the young, new families forming among wage earners between 25 and 35 years old. The number of homeowners in this group declined by more than 7 percent. Millions of young people whose older brothers and sisters had purchased homes at the same age were squeezed out of the market. Many will never manage to catch up.

Nothing conveys more dramatically the skewed values of the conservative order that reigned during the 1980s than the two competing realities: On one hand, disastrous events in the private financial system forced the federal government into the awkward role of real estate magnate—the bloated owner and landlord of thousands of vacant private homes and commercial properties of every kind. On the other hand, there is a housing shortage. The private marketplace, following its own free-market incentives, simply failed to build enough new housing to provide shelter for people of moderate means. This was not an accident. It was made possible, if not inevitable, when politicians of both parties agreed to deregulate the financial system.

In fact, what happened is consistent with what the advocates of deregulation said they wanted. When the banking industry lobbied for financial deregulation in the 1970s, one of its favorite arguments was that America had been misallocating its scarce capital, devoting too much of it to housing. The interest-rate ceilings in federal regulations made the cost of home mortgages unnaturally cheap.

That subsidy for borrowers, combined with others embedded in the tax code, led the private economy to build more and larger houses than the country really needed. If these artificial advantages for housing were eliminated, the lobbyists contended, the nation could devote more of its savings to expanding productive capacity, and everyone would benefit. In the end, they won the argument, and political controls were repealed. Ten years later, we can see the consequences on city sidewalks all around us.

The old social contract, popularly articulated since World War II as the American dream, was set aside.

Finance is an essential strand in the social contract, though neither economists nor financiers like to think about it in those terms. The political boundaries governing the financial system are inescapably a statement of shared values, the social premises that almost everyone accepts and supports. When the rules of banking and credit were altered, so were its social purposes. The old social contract, popularly articulated since World War II as the American dream, was set aside and replaced by a harsher version.

In suburban Virginia, outside the nation's capital, an official at the new homeless shelter in Reston explained how the shelter's clientele was changing. "We're seeing a large number of people who lose their housing because they can't keep up with the rent," Jana Graves said. "They may be working, even at two jobs, making $10,000 to $12,000 a year, and something happens—an illness or they lose a job—and they end up in the shelter."

Initially, at least, the increased number of urban homeless was dismissed as an unintended side effect of deinstitutionalizing the mentally ill. By the late 1980s it was obvious to anyone willing to look that something larger was at work. City streets and community shelters were now occupied by thousands of homeless families with children and increasing proportions of adults who actually went to work every day at low-paying service jobs but who couldn't afford local rents. Typically, the homeless often have other personal problems—alcoholism or drug abuse or family disruptions—which allow many people to rationalize the problem: in effect, to blame the victims. But if alcoholism or drug addiction had made these people homeless, then why were there so few homeless people on the city streets 10 years ago? There were no fewer alcoholics or drug addicts in the 1970s than there were in the 1980s. But there was a more ample supply of housing, even the marginal sort where the poorest, most hapless citizens could find shelter.

The new shelter in Reston turned away more than a thousand people in its first nine months of operation in 1988. On the night I visited there, 21 of its 60 beds were occupied by children. A young mother was showing off her "shelter baby," an infant who had never lived anywhere else. One resident, a young black man who worked at a service station and was living in the back of his van, lost his home when the van was totaled in an accident. A friend got him a bed at the public shelter.

The squeeze on affordable housing extended across a much broader front than just the poor people out on the streets or those who were paying outrageous rents for slum dwellings. The middle class felt the pressure too. Especially hard hit were those people who worked in the community but because of soaring home prices could no longer afford to live there. "Our policemen, our firemen, our schoolteachers are forced to live an hour out of town," Dwight Schar, a homebuilder in Fairfax, Virginia, lamented. "That changes the character of the community."

The homeless and the middle class are people of very different means and circumstances, yet they are all bound up in essentially the same problem: the U.S. did not build enough affordable new housing in the past decade to accommodate the enormous upsurge in new families, the famous population bulge known as the baby boom. Everyone is now compelled to cope with the consequences of scarcity. At the very least, all will wind up paying inflated prices, whether they are buyers or renters, whether well-to-do or poor.

The housing market has always functioned in a classic trickle-down fashion. When a prospering young couple can afford for the first time to buy a new house, they usually move up-market to what homebuilders call a starter home. That purchase vacates the house or apartment they had been renting, and someone else a bit down the ladder moves up to fill it. The chain continues in this manner until the new vacancy has moved down to the very bottom of the housing market—the least desirable parts of town where the poor people live. Thus, if the natural demand for new housing is suppressed, as it was by the high real interest rates of the 1980s, a negative wave backs its way down through the entire market. When the young middle-class couple can't afford to move up to a starter home, the new house doesn't get built, and they continue to rent. That keeps rental vacancies scarce, and rents rise everywhere, even in the nastiest slums. It is the law of supply and demand with a vengeance.

The crucial question is what caused the housing market to fall short of meeting the demand for new housing? Many different factors had depressed the housing market of the 1980s, but one was central and more damaging than any other: the extraordinarily high cost of borrowing for home mortgages. Mortgage rates were also effectively liberated in the deregulation of finance, and, not surprisingly, creditors demanded more for the use of their money now that they were legally free to do so. The effects of deregulation were compounded by the Federal Reserve's campaign against inflation and its willingness to hold real interest rates at unprecedented levels throughout the decade. When the Reagan administration virtually stopped construction of subsidized housing for low-income families, the squeeze on the poor was tightened further.

Like other aspects of the financial system, the true cost of mortgage borrowing has been grossly obscured by political mythology.

Like other aspects of the financial system, the true cost of mortgage borrowing has been grossly obscured by political mythology. Ronald Reagan and other Republicans continually celebrated the decline of interest rates during their tenure and reminded voters of the bad old days when Jimmy Carter was president and mortgage rates went through the roof. Most home-buyers, looking at nominal interest rates, agreed that things were much better, when in fact things were much worse. In terms of the real interest costs—the nominal rate minus the inflation rate—home-buyers were paying many times more for their mortgages in the 1980s.

Lenders understand this, even if borrowers do not. An 11 percent mortgage in 1979 was very cheap because general price inflation was running at roughly the same level. The real interest cost in the late 1970s was usually less than 1 percent and was often even negative. The same 11 percent mortgage a few years later carried a real interest rate of 6 or 8 percent because inflation had fallen. By the end of the

INFLATION-ADJUSTED MORTGAGE RATES

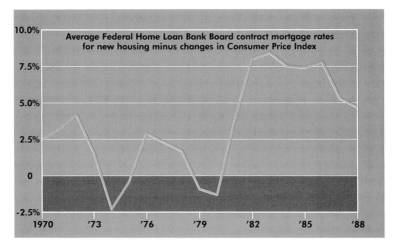

SOURCES: OFFICE OF THRIFT SUPERVISION; U.S. DEPARTMENT OF LABOR

4:13 PM, Memphis, Tennessee. Incoming calls are handled.

Our main Call Center handles more than 260,000 calls per day.
Wherever you are, Federal Express is only a phone call away.

decade, this was still true: the nominal interest rates on mortgages were below their record peaks of the early Eighties, but the real cost of home financing was outrageously more expensive.

The lenders, in other words, were enjoying a margin of return that was three or four times greater, in real terms, and the borrowers were struggling to keep up with the monthly payments. The first consequence was to price millions of potential buyers out of the single-family home market—a big chunk of the baby-boom generation. Their predicament was aggravated, of course, by the maldistribution of wages and wealth, which shifted income shares of the wealthy upward on the ladder while the bottom 40 percent of the population suffered real decline. Millions of families stretched their budgets and took on the increased burden of higher real mortgage rates, paying a much larger share of their incomes for housing. Many of them didn't make it, which helps to explain why the default rates on home mortgages continued at record levels throughout the decade, despite the supposed prosperity. Once these economic forces were at work on the housing market, perverse consequences unfolded. Homebuilders, for instance, soon grasped that the market for new homes was moving upscale, and they moved with it. Kent Colton, executive vice-president of the National Association of Home Builders, estimated that two-thirds of the new homes were built for the pricey upper end of the market, while the construction of modestly priced starter homes shrank by nearly half. That naturally exacerbated the problem of inadequate housing supply for families of modest means and at the same time produced a national surplus of luxury homes.

For the poor, the tensions were even worse. Rents increased fastest at the lowest end of the housing market, according to a 1988 study by the Joint Center for Housing Studies at Harvard University, because the supply squeeze intensified at the bottom. Old inner-city dwellings got gentrified or torn down to make way for new buildings—more than one million low-rent units disappeared during the decade—while the number of poor families competing for the worst housing simultaneously increased. The losers in this competition wound up in shelters or on the street.

Obviously, a substantial shift in public policies will be required to overcome these shortages and reverse the deterioration. But the federal government is proceeding to make things worse. As the Federal Reserve pushed interest rates up from 6.5 to nearly 10 percent in 1988 and 1989 in order to slow the economy, the first casualty was, as usual, housing. Every 1 percent increase in mortgage rates drives 1.7 million potential home-buyers out of the market, according to Michael Sumichrast, former chief economist of the National Association of Home Builders. The Urban Institute estimates that the nation must build 1.9 million new housing units a year to keep up with the need, but the Federal Reserve's decision to tighten credit has the opposite result. The higher rates depressed the homebuilding industry to an annual production level of about 1.4 million units—that is, a 500,000 shortfall in available housing units. Under those conditions, the housing crisis is sure to worsen.

The higher rates also deepen the cracks in the financial system by provoking more defaults on existing mortgages. As the Fed tightens, homeowners who bought in with variable-rate mortgages see their monthly payments climb, and some cannot keep up. Indeed, in the less prosperous regions of the country, many of the housing defaults were attributed to homeowners who simply walked away, once they realized, after years of payments, that they had accumulated virtually no equity of their own. Housing prices did not appreciate in their areas, and thanks to the high interest rates, their monthly payments were devoted almost entirely to paying interest.

The surge in defaults, in turn, begins to threaten the balance sheets of the lenders, such as the Federal Housing Administration (FHA), which insures $275 billion in mortgages on medium-priced homes. Having suffered losses for two years, the FHA's reserve had dwindled to $2.8 billion by the middle of 1989—barely enough to cover default claims for five months of losses. If the FHA goes broke, of course, the taxpayers will be obliged to make it whole, whatever the cost. The same threat confronts other lending agencies, both public and private.

The old social contract promised that an increasing number of people would be able to buy homes, and for a time that promise was honored. For two generations, Americans could see it with their own eyes. Home ownership became an attainable goal for an ever-widening circle of people. It meant pride and stability and lots of other worthy social values. It also mildly redistributed wealth to the homeowners and aided financial self-sufficiency across a very broad range of Americans. Owning a home, paying off the mortgage, and accumulating the appreciating value represented the only means that most families had of storing up any significant wealth of their own. Home ownership was the bedrock of society's promise to itself.

In the era of financial deregulation, that social standard has deteriorated, and for many people it no longer exists. It is now more accurate to say that home ownership is no longer considered a prerogative of the middle class below a certain level of earnings. In fact, the new social contract appears to hold that some citizens, those who do not possess an acceptable level of income, are entitled to no shelter at all.

T he backbone of the nation's longstanding commitment to home ownership was the savings and loan industry, the principal mortgage lender for many years. The government protected it against its larger competitors and provided a modest rate advantage to ensure that it would always have ample deposit funds for home lending. For more than 40 years, the arrangement generally worked. Home-buyers enjoyed a modest hidden subsidy, and except for during episodes of tight money, most working people could obtain a mortgage. The 1980 legislation, amid the rhetoric of free-market efficiency, removed those privileges. The S&L industry would now be "freed" to compete with commercial banks and others. Albert Wojnilower of First Boston observed at the time: "Freeing the thrift and mortgage markets from government subsidy and guarantee is like freeing family pets by abandoning them in the jungle."

The driving political force for financial deregulation was not laissez-faire theories of economic efficiency or arguments about integrating with the global financial system. It was financial-sector politics combined with double-digit inflation. Commercial banks had waged a 15-year campaign against the Federal Reserve's famous Regulation Q, which set interest-rate ceilings and differentials, and banks had succeeded in peeling off rate controls on one financial instrument after another. Each time the regulators gave in to the bankers, the remaining controls were weakened because there were more opportunities to evade them.

The *coup de grâce* that killed off Regulation Q, however, was inflation. The S&Ls were crippled by it, because as market interest rates rose, their balance sheets were turned upside down—they had lent long-term at fixed rates but were now borrowing short-term at higher rates. If they didn't borrow, they couldn't lend. Their depositors left for other places, especially the money-market mutual funds invented by Wall Street investment houses, where their savings would draw higher rates.

Furthermore, the once equitable social deal embedded in the preferential treatment for savings and loans now seemed badly skewed. The earnest mom-and-pop depositors who kept modest savings accounts at their local thrifts had become victims of the system. The virtuous "small saver"—a widow or family of humble means whose savings were losing real value because of inflation, yet still collected artificially low interest rates because of Regulation Q—was invoked in the political debate. Larger and more savvy players enjoyed much greater returns in the money market. Justice demanded market rates for everyone, or so it was said at the time. When the Gray Panthers came out for financial deregulation, the long political argument was essentially settled.

Having read nearly all of the congressional debate surrounding the financial deregulation of 1980, I was struck, first, by the fact that housing was barely mentioned. It was as though the liberal Democrats who supported deregulation did not want to remind themselves that they were undoing one of the great achievements of the New Deal era.

The second fundamental point missing from the debate was the contradiction that has led to so much financial destruction. The S&Ls would now be treated like grown-ups—freed to compete head-on with larger, more skillful financial adversaries—and surely that increased the likelihood that many would fail. The debate acknowledged as much. Yet Congress not only kept the same lenient rules for federal deposit insurance but also jacked up the coverage substantially, from $40,000 to $100,000 deposits. Kenneth A. Guenther, executive vice-president of the Independent Bankers Association of America, observed: "The combination of interest-rate deregulation with 100 percent deposit insurance is like the invention of gunpowder—sooner or later it was bound to explode."

To Kenneth A. Guenther of the Independent Bankers Association of America, the combination of deregulation and deposit insurance "was bound to explode."

The resulting wreckage is now fully visible. Everyone, in both politics and finance, has dirty hands. Instead of schooling the thrifts to live prudently in their harsh new environment, the Reagan administration encouraged the opposite, first by drastically cutting back regulatory supervision and then by advocating new lending powers for the embattled S&Ls, allowing them to try their luck in the tricky realms of commercial lending.

Wall Street also played its part. Merrill Lynch and Company Inc. inventively initiated "brokered deposits," in which vast billions from large-scale investors would be sliced up into $100,000 packages and parceled out by computer to S&Ls. These were jumbo deposits that were fully covered by federal insurance, regardless of whether the S&Ls were sound. Many were insolvent, and the brokers knew it. Other firms picked up the game, and soon thrift managers were enjoying ample funding with which to make their disastrously bad loans. Merrill Lynch and other big brokerages are now finding profit on the other end of the process too, as they prepare for a lively business buying and selling the government-owned carcasses.

The Federal Reserve also deserves more blame than it has been given for the S&L debacle. When Paul Volcker was steering his tough-minded monetary policy, he was warned repeatedly by colleagues and staff economists that whatever his goals for the overall economy might be, there would be expensive consequences if he did not moderate and allow interest rates to fall. Volcker mostly ignored this advice, but that doesn't mean it was wrong. One former Fed economist told me that, early on, the staff predicted privately that given the level of interest rates the Federal Reserve was imposing on the economy, something like 800 savings and loans would eventually fail. Years later, it looks like a reasonably accurate, if not too conservative, forecast.

The broken wheel has not been fixed. The 1989 savings and loan bailout legislation did impose new restraints on the thrift industry, especially by setting more rigorous capital standards. By putting more of the S&Ls' own money at risk, the higher capital requirements may make many S&L managers behave more prudently. But the result could well be the opposite; a higher capital base did not prevent the major commercial bankers from plunging into various swamps, such as third-world debt, from which the government had to extricate them. Several years earlier, when federal regulators were raising capital requirements for the banks, Albert Wojnilower observed: "The only way for most intermediaries to earn a competitive return on a higher capital base is by raising the average lending margin, and that can be accomplished only by making riskier loans. Any apparent gain to the soundness of the financial structure as a whole is illusory."

Nor, beyond an embarrassed nod, did the bailout legislation acknowledge the housing crisis that is the social analogue of the financial crisis. Housing and homelessness are not fixed either and won't be soon. The creation of the Resolution Trust Corporation is a scandal waiting to happen. The deeper problems will not be truly mended until there is a general reform of the rules governing finance. Since neither Congress nor the president was prepared to take an honest look at the real damage wrought by the era of deregulation, they were naturally not prepared to consider real reforms. Perhaps, if even more spectacular failures lie ahead, the continuing shock and loss will eventually open their minds.

12:15 AM, Memphis, Tennessee. Packages sorted at main hub.

In less than two hours, the Federal Express hub system processes more than one million packages per night.

5:21 PM, Montreal, Quebec. Supertracker records package location.

To verify the location of your packages, the Federal Express Supertracker® enters the data into our computerized COSMOS tracking system.

MORAL HAZARD

The representative man of the 1980s, aside from Ronald Reagan himself, was undoubtedly Michael Milken, formerly of Drexel Burnham Lambert, the inventive financier who recognized possibilities ahead of the crowd and became a fabulous pioneer. Like Reagan, Milken is an optimist beyond the normal bounds, a man who was willing to brush aside the niggling details that inhibit less adventurous souls and put his full faith in the future. As with Reagan's management of the federal government, optimism was the essence of the vast deals that Milken engineered, issuing billions in junk bonds and using the proceeds to buy up major corporations. Things will work out, Milken assured the doubters, if only you have the vision to trust the abundant future of American enterprise. Things did work out for Milken, at least until his indictment in March of 1989. His faith was rewarded one year with a pioneering income of $550 million, surely the highest annual compensation paid for one man's labor in the whole history of capitalism.

Immediate gratification was the other essential premise of Milken's complex financial enterprises. Everyone else—workers, managers, and shareholders—should place his faith in the future, but the initiating investors would be rewarded *right now*. This, as it happens, was exactly the mix—optimism and immediate gratification—that Ronald Reagan brought to the federal budget process with such great political success. The federal government would spend the money on things it wanted now and trust the future to pay for them. The same principle, applied so energetically to corporate America by Milken and others, is now reflected on hundreds of balance sheets. Business is in debt at an unprecedented level.

The process of recapitalization and restructuring that Milken championed was not new to American corporate capitalism. When it

Optimism and immediate gratification formed the essence of the vast junk-bond deals engineered by Michael Milken.

was pursued before on a vast scale, in the 1920s, the practice of issuing huge blocks of new stock in a company without increasing its value was known as watering stock. In both episodes, the consequences—weakened corporate structures—were the same because the objective was the same: to extract the capital invested in the underutilized real assets of the corporations so that the money could be redeployed in higher yielding financial instruments. It is another dramatic example of how finance has triumphed over the real economy. Why own a factory when your capital will draw a better real return from paper?

Aside from Milken's ingenuity, the fundamental force driving the frenzy of takeovers in the 1980s was the high level of real interest rates. If a company's factories and other assets could not match the return, they would be cannibalized. As long as real interest rates remained at extraordinary levels, as they did through both the 1920s and the 1980s (see chart, page 70), the incentive to disassemble corporations would be irresistible.

In the short term, nearly everyone seems to win in these maneuvers (except, of course, the displaced workers). Shareholders get a premium price, and the new owners get control. The dealers reap astounding fees, and even the ousted management gets bought off with lucrative compensation. But the long-term survival of the corporation is threatened when it becomes saddled with an un-natural burden of debt. As long as the corporation thrives, management may hope to keep up with the monthly payments. When the economy contracts, though, many of those corporations will discover that a different future has evolved, one that features debt default and bankruptcy.

The deleterious effects of junk-bond debt on American corporations have been argued and reargued as the takeover deals grow larger and larger. The debt has deflected companies from long-term research and development. It has leveraged cash flow to a higher degree than was the case even at the depths of the 1982 recession. It encourages tighter management control of costs, to be sure, but it also frequently destroys viable productive capacity and, of course, the accompanying jobs. Most perversely, it leads healthy companies to acquire protective layers of debt, deliberately distorting their balance sheets so that they will be unattractive to potential raiders.

What is not so well understood is the financial risk—the fact that the proliferation of takeovers and the accompanying debt is also a direct threat to the stability of the whole financial system. Once again, the ultimate liability is unwittingly held by the American taxpayers, not by the financiers who brokered the arrangements. If economic conditions eventually produce a wave of defaults in junk bonds, the investors enjoying their high yields will suffer losses, but the defaults will also cascade through the banking system. The government will once again be obligated to rescue the major losers.

Martin Lipton, a New York lawyer who acts as a legal adviser in takeover battles, sounded a jeremiad in the strongest terms. "Our nation is blindly rushing toward the precipice," Lipton warned in a 1988 newsletter to his firm's blue-chip clients. "As with tulip bulbs, South Sea bubbles, pyramid investment trusts, Florida land, REITs [real estate investment trusts], LDC [less-developed country] loans, Texas banks, and all the other financial-market frenzies of the past, the denouement will be a crash. We and our children will pay a gigantic price for allowing abusive takeover tactics and bootstrap, junk-bond takeovers."

Federal Reserve chairman Alan Greenspan has expressed his anxieties about the potential "shock" that might occur from junk-bond failures, as has Treasury secretary Nicholas Brady. To do anything serious to avert this threat, however, would require them to make a frank break with the laissez-faire ethos. Neither the Fed nor the Treasury, nor the president for that matter, seems up to challenging the orthodoxy so directly.

Congress itself became slightly more sensitive to the risk when it was legislating the 1989 savings and loan bailout. A relatively small number of savings and loans, led by Milken's old friends like Thomas Spiegel, chairman of Columbia Savings and Loan Association in Beverly Hills, California, held large portfolios of junk bonds themselves. Columbia had one-third of its assets, $3.9 billion, in the high-yield paper in 1988. Overall, 8 percent of outstanding junk bonds—$14.4 billion—were owned by federally insured S&Ls. Congress decided that it would be prudent for the S&Ls to back out of that field of risk-taking, but gradually, by 1994, so as not to collapse prices and endanger others.

In fact, commercial banks are exposed to the same risks because they have been the major lenders of the mergers-and-acquisitions movement, and their lending is probably even larger than the junk-bond market. If one fails, both fail. If a corporation sinks under its swollen debts, it will not be able to pay off the bank loans either.

Kohlberg, Kravis, Roberts & Company, the investment firm that managed some of the largest leveraged buyouts (LBOs), has estimated that commercial bank loans make up about 40 percent of the typical LBO debt package. Others think that the proportion is higher. A study by the Securities and Exchange Commission estimated that 57 percent of the credit in these deals comes from the banks. According to *Barron's*, merger-related lending by commercial banks soared from $3 billion in early 1984 to $115.5 billion in late 1988—a spectacular increase.

Of course, it is good business for the banks, as long as Milken's kind of optimism prevails. If the markets falter, the major banks will be at risk on two fronts: they lent capital directly for takeover deals, and they provided liquidity lending to major Wall Street brokerages that also financed takeovers. A study by the Brookings Institution concluded that given the buildup of corporate debt, 10 percent of the country's public corporations would go bankrupt if a recession as severe as the one in 1973-74 developed. The financial damage could be quickly compounded if nervous investors began dumping their junk bonds or, worse, found that there were no willing buyers. In either case, the Fed would have to step forward as the lender of last resort and start bailing out banks and brokerages.

The Federal Reserve was concerned enough by this possibility to issue its own warning memorandum to bank supervisors in early

Given the buildup of corporate debt, 10 percent of the country's public corporations would go bankrupt if a recession as severe as the one in 1973-74 developed.

1989, asking them to take a careful look at how banks are exposed in highly leveraged financial deals. The National Association of Manufacturers (NAM), whose members are the prime targets in the takeover game, urged the Fed and the Treasury to take stronger action, given "the potential economic disaster of large-scale defaults during a recession."

In June of 1989, Jerry J. Jasinowski, NAM's president and chief economist, wrote to the Treasury secretary: "We suggest the Federal Reserve study the possibility of prohibiting federal-bank participation in takeover and corporate-control situations if the principal does not have a required percentage of unencumbered equity in the initial transaction." In other words, stop the deals in which a player can take over a company with no money down—at least none of his own.

Junk bonds represent only one of several new dimensions of risk that are generally unrecognized by the public but threaten the stability of the financial system. The collapse of major banks and the savings and loan bailout have gradually educated both politicians and voters on their exposure to loss from conventional bank lending. Next, if things go badly, the American people may learn painfully about other, more esoteric forms of public obligation.

 mong the many marvelous innovations made possible by computerization, the financial system has developed one that makes bankers disappear. It is called securitization, and it has spawned vast markets that barely existed a decade ago. The practice was first established with home mortgages; thousands of them were bundled together in large packages for resale to general investors as mortgage-backed securities. That way, the initiating lender—a bank or an S&L—could execute the mortgages, then offload them on the secondary market and go out and make more. Now, the same technique is being applied to many other kinds of credit, including business lending: bundles of loans are being sold by the basketful to financial markets.

Without question, securitization improves efficiency, for it requires the standardization of loan terms so that loans can be easily bound together in one bond. Some academics think that this is the big wave of the future: a financial world in which nearly all kinds of loans are made in standard formats, easily bundled, and resold wholesale to investors. In the new age, borrowers will be able to stop by the drive-in loan window in the local shopping center, much as they now drop off their film at the photo kiosk. Those old, monumental, and forbidding bank buildings, meant to evoke a

Those old, forbidding bank buildings are already thoroughly passé in the age of securitization.

sense of trust and authority, are already thoroughly passé.

The problem with securitization, as federal regulators have come to realize, is that the friendly banker disappears too. Traditionally, he was the authority who kept an eye on the borrowers and disciplined them, who prescribed stern remedies when they got in over their heads. In the securitized world, the banker moves on to other clients, having little interest in tending to his old loans, since they've already been packaged and sold in the marketplace. The new creditors—the pension funds or money-market funds or other banks or private citizens who bought the securities—know little about the borrowers who are on the other end of these transactions.

So who's minding the store? The question nags federal bank

Henry Kaufman, formerly of Salomon Brothers: "In a securitized world, the Fed will inherit the problem of the troublesome debtor."

regulators because, in the end, it will be they who must step in and clean up the mess. E. Gerald Corrigan, president of the New York Federal Reserve Bank, lamented in an important essay about financial regulation that the "credit watchdog," or the supervising banker, was now essentially absent from a huge volume of credit transactions. "Looking at the stability of the system," Corrigan wrote, "the continuous association of the bank with the debtor—including the 'workout' of problem situations—is just as central to the credit decision-making process as the initial extension of credit....The bank's role as the originator and holder of credit to high-quality borrowers has been significantly undercut."

Henry Kaufman, former chief economist at Salomon Brothers Inc., put the problem in terms that explain why Federal Reserve officials are worried: "Securitization...tends to create the illusion that credit risk can be reduced by the marketability of the credit instruments. The risk is that the disciplining force involved in the relationship between creditor and debtor is loosened because creditors are not permanent holders of the debt....In a securitized world, the Fed will inherit the problem of the troublesome debtor...."

These are theoretical problems, and without an actual, visible calamity to confirm what authorities like Corrigan and Kaufman are saying, it is virtually impossible to convince nonexperts to take them seriously. The nonexperts might also be unmoved by the knowledge that in substantial measure the securitized markets are directly guaranteed by the American taxpayers. This is so because the securities-marketing corporations that operate in these markets are hybrid creatures called government-sponsored enterprises (GSEs). They are private corporations, but when they borrow money in financial markets, investors correctly presume that the bonds are backed by the federal government.

The best known of the GSEs is Fannie Mae, the Federal National Mortgage Association. Others have cute names like Freddie Mac, Sallie Mae, and Farmer Mac. All were created to provide secondary markets for debt paper for such worthy purposes as student loans and farm mortgages. Collectively, they have been growing rapidly—at a rate of 18 percent a year since 1970; together they hold a staggering total of $720 billion in debt. Lately Congress has been creating new GSEs to finance bailouts. A virtue of government-sponsored enterprises that especially appeals to politicians is that GSEs can borrow and spend money without the debt's showing up on the official federal budget.

"Government-sponsored enterprises," Washington attorney

8:00 AM, New York City. Walk-in Service Center opens for business.

Federal Express has fully-staffed service centers
in more than 1400 locations throughout the world.

Thomas H. Stanton warned in a 1989 congressional hearing, "combine the two potentially explosive ingredients contributing to the financial collapse of the Federal Savings and Loan Insurance Corporation: an open-ended extension of federal credit support to private financial institutions, and a failure to properly regulate the safety and soundness of those institutions."

The fundamental issue, Stanton explained, is what economists like to call moral hazard, an economic incentive to seek greater returns by taking on extraordinary risks because someone else will be responsible for the losses. Moral hazard is the issue that lies across the entire financial system, from the deregulated banks to junk bonds. For the government-sponsored corporations, it means the ability to put up little private capital and assume huge obligations because the U.S. Treasury is standing close by. Fannie Mae, for instance, in 1989 had only $2.6 billion in shareholder equity behind $196.5 billion in combined assets. Freddie Mac had only $1.7 billion supporting $278 billion. The normal market discipline of investors checking out a company before they buy stock doesn't apply, Stanton warned, because everyone understands the arrangement. "Heads, the corporation and its shareholders win. Tails, the U.S. taxpayer pays for the big mistakes."

Henry Kaufman and others warned long ago about what was unfolding in the era of relaxed regulation of finance, and now it is fully visible. "This growth in credit is nourished by...the willingness of our government to spread an official safety net over a variety of participants, which tends to reduce the risk of borrowing," he said. "No large business corporation is allowed to fail. No large financial institution is allowed to fail. No institution that has depositors is allowed to fail in its obligations to depositors, large or small. Federal credit agencies that get into difficulty are not allowed to fail. So there is a kind of official safety net that's spreading and that is perceived by the marketplace."

Where does the moral hazard come to rest? Not in the financial markets, but in Washington.

eneral Electric Company is Kidder, Peabody Group Inc.; Ford Motor Company is First Nationwide Financial Corporation; Sears, Roebuck and Company is Dean Witter Reynolds Inc. The last frontier of financial deregulation, erasing the boundaries between commerce and banking, is still being explored despite misgivings about what has already happened in the name of freeing markets. Commercial banks, feeling their own turf squeezed on many fronts, are pushing in one direction, trying to win political approval to invade other fields like insurance and the stock-brokerage business. Industrial and retail corporations are at the same time building a substantial presence in finance, wedging their way into the bankers' domain.

If banks can get into any kind of business, then every business will have to become a bank.

As former senator William Proxmire once observed, if banks can get into any kind of business, then every business will have to become a bank. There is an obvious conflict of interest if the distributors of credit, the banks that decide which businesses are worthy borrowers, have their own horses entered in the race. The corollary to Proxmire's theorem is that if Ford Motor Company or General Motors Corporation owns a major bank, then federal regulators may decide that those companies are also too big to fail.

The regulation of banking and allied financial activities becomes less and less rational each year as the banks and competing businesses discover more loopholes. The process is now so far advanced that many legislators who once believed in holding the line by keeping these separations intact are now prepared to let it go. They propose building "fire walls" within corporations so that the banking component could be kept separate from the rest. This is the newest version of wishful thinking.

Commercial banks were excluded from investment banking and other financial activities by the famous Glass-Steagall Act of 1933, but the division between commerce and banking is as old as the Republic. Both kinds of legal barriers have important implications for the future soundness of the banking system, but the most crucial is the tradition that prevents regular business firms from becoming banks and vice versa. Gerald Corrigan explained why: "We may be approaching a point where, as a practical matter, the distinction between banking and commerce could be irreversibly breached. If that point is reached, it potentially implies, as a matter of logic, that, first, either the 'safety net' surrounding banking will have to be extended...to those who own and control banks or, second, that the 'safety net' should be eliminated altogether...."

Corrigan, for one, is skeptical that one division of a company— the bank—can truly be operated independently of the whole, especially if one or the other should get into difficulty. "Absent such independence," he wrote, "concerns about conflicts of interest, unfair competition, concentration of economic power, and breaches of fiduciary responsibilities can only increase sharply."

The bottom line is another form of moral hazard. The de facto protective fence that has been spread wider and wider across the landscape of financial services could be extended further, to nonfinancial businesses. Conceivably, this has already happened as industrial corporations and retailers buy into Wall Street brokerages and the so-called nonbank banks. Would the Federal Reserve someday open its "discount window" to Ford or Sears in the interest of protecting the banking system?

Down the road a way, perhaps too late, the corporations that want so much to become financiers may realize that the plan was not a good bargain, after all. Eventually, when the public catches on and the political climate shifts, there will be a general reregulation of the financial system. Companies that have made themselves into banks and are riding free on the government regulators' protection may find that they are also subject to the government regulators' supervision.

For the nation as a whole, the coupling of federal protection with nonfinancial corporations suggests a dark prospect for what might eventually emerge in the American political system. It could amount to a corporatist state in which the government's vast powers are devoted primarily to protecting the fortunes of the elite, a relative handful of very large conglomerate corporations, while smaller enterprises are left to struggle with the perils of freedom. Some doleful critics would argue that this system is already in place.

ll of these various strands of complex financial risk ultimately wind up on one doorstep—the Federal Reserve's. As the regulator of money, the ultimate guarantor of safety and soundness, and the lender of last resort, the Fed must manage the crisis, if one develops from any of these potentialities. Yet, as manager of the economy, the Fed is also occasionally called on to impose discipline on private enterprise in the form of higher interest rates and slower growth, even by inducing a recession.

Its actions in one realm threaten to unravel the other. If the central bank forces the issue on inflation and growth, it may find itself swamped with casualties in the deregulated banking system. All of the profound contradictions in the present order of money come together at the Fed.

5:00 PM, Paris, France. Pick-up near Eiffel Tower.

Federal Express serves more than 99% of the U.S. population
and is already helping business in Western Europe prepare for 1992.

THE BLOODLETTING

I n the middle of 1989, as he watched the effects of tight money squeeze his company's balance sheet, the chairman and CEO of Eastman Kodak felt an uncomfortable sense of *déjà vu*. "One of the things that I can't help but see," Colby H. Chandler said, "is that we're going through an experience that feels and sounds just like the early part of the Eighties."

Economists in New York and Washington assured him that this was not so. The higher interest rates engineered by the Federal Reserve over the previous year would subside, producing a "soft landing," not a full-blown contraction, for the domestic economy. And, they added, the dollar—up 15 to 20 percent on foreign-exchange markets since the Fed had pushed up interest rates—would not continue to appreciate. Chandler assumed that they were correct; he certainly hoped they were.

But then the Kodak chairman remembered that economists had given him the same assurances, year after year, the last time the Fed had kept the brake on the economy. American manufacturing had been devastated as a consequence. Starting in 1981, Chandler recalled, economists had predicted every year that the rising dollar would "turn around" the next year. Yet each time they had renewed their prediction, the dollar went still higher. Finally, by 1985, the forecast came true—four years late. In the interim, Eastman Kodak had lost between $3.5 billion and $4 billion in earnings.

This time, Colby Chandler was alarmed enough by the drift of events to voice his anxieties in a public plea to the Federal Reserve. MR. GREENSPAN, LOWER RATES NOW! read the headline on his article in *The New York Times*' Sunday business section. "Higher interest rates are the last thing this country needs," Chandler wrote. "Higher interest rates will force American industry to forgo investment or to move it offshore. The American economy needs much more investment, not less, yet our current policies will guarantee that we continue to underinvest in our economic future."

Eastman Kodak, a familiar old name in American manufacturing, is still based in its hometown of Rochester, New York. But the company long ago became a modern multinational, selling photo-

The way the money system now works to control inflation constitutes a de facto system for the gradual deindustrialization of the American economy.

graphic film, copiers, and other high-tech products around the world. 1988 was a very good year for Kodak. Like other export manufacturers, it was still recovering briskly from the terrible years of the overvalued dollar, and Kodak's fast-growing export business had provided about 44 percent of its $17 billion in sales. Net earnings were $1.4 billion, up 19 percent. The company's managers had every reason to expect the same for 1989.

The central bank, urged on by opinion in the financial markets, made a decision that doomed that expectation. Kodak found itself embattled again by the summer of 1989, watching its profit margin shrink steadily while Wall Street stock-market analysts nagged the company to cut costs to make up for the disappointing earnings. Kodak is not a company that economists would describe as interest-sensitive like housing or automobiles, the industries that always absorb the heaviest damage from tight monetary policy. Families do not need a bank loan to buy film for their cameras, nor usually do companies that are purchasing office equipment. But when the Federal Reserve pushed interest rates up from 6.5 percent to nearly 10 percent, as it did from March of 1988 to April of 1989, the shock went right to Kodak's bottom line. "I don't think a company can escape it," Chandler said. "A lot of people may think they can, but I don't think so."

Traditionally, captains of industry raised no objections when the Federal Reserve imposed a recession on the economy, even though it would temporarily depress their own sales and profits. Indeed, industrialists often discreetly cheered the Fed on, and many still do. Whatever short-term discomforts resulted, the Fed's action gave corporate managers powerful leverage over their old nemesis, labor. High unemployment pushed wages down and undermined the unions' bargaining power. Recessions were regarded as an opportunity to cut costs, especially labor costs.

But in the modern global economy of the 1980s, the supposed benefit of smashing labor had become increasingly less valuable to corporate balance sheets, at least in manufacturing. U.S. industrial wages were already falling in real terms. Labor unions were already decimated. What endured, however, was the damage to companies themselves. Some corporate executives—not many, but a few— were beginning to grasp that the governing system for money exacts more than transitory costs. In fact, the way the money system now works to control inflation constitutes a de facto system for the gradual deindustrialization of the American economy.

When the Federal Reserve started pushing interest rates up again in the spring of 1988, the first inescapable cost for Kodak was on its own borrowing. Like any major corporation, Kodak borrows huge amounts short-term in the money market—about $2.6 billion a year—to manage its cash flow and as part of its overall debt structure of $10.4 billion. An additional toll of 3 percent interest, charged on $2.6 billion, was not small change. Furthermore, as long as rates stayed up, the company would have to abandon its goal of shifting more of its debt from short-term to long-term obligations, from variable rates to fixed rates.

Kodak also felt the pressure building among its customers. A fierce little contest developed between buyers and sellers over who would get stuck with the cost of the higher interest rates. "One thing you will notice," Chandler explained, "is that our inventories and our receivables both went up considerably in 1988—each about

Colby H. Chandler of Eastman Kodak: "The stronger dollar makes our goods overseas either not marketable, or we have to lower our prices. In Europe we had an interval of time with no earnings."

$500 million. That's a big cost to a company like Kodak. There's a billion dollars there, and the cost to us is the cost of that float."

Nearly all of Kodak's direct sales are to other businesses, whether to retail stores selling film or to insurance companies buying office machines. All of those customers felt the same cost squeeze as interest rates rose. "I think it's inevitable as you get tighter money—everybody tries to push the financial load either onto suppliers or a customer," Chandler explained. "You try to move it, and you negotiate very, very hard. The supplier ends up carrying more inventory because the user will say, 'I want to continue to buy the same quantity from you, but you keep it, and I'll tell you when I want it.' That means that you have to carry inventory for their ups and downs, which is a cost. On the receivables, they'll stretch [them] as long as they can. They'll try for longer terms, and you'll find those creeping up from 60 days to 70 days and perhaps longer."

These balance-sheet problems were costly but minor compared with what happened to Kodak in the global marketplace. The company's sales remained buoyant, but earnings shrank. The explanation was not mysterious: as the Fed drove up U.S. interest rates, global investors seeking the highest return put more of their money into dollar-denominated financial assets. The increased demand for dollars, in turn, bid up the international exchange value of the dollar.

"The stronger dollar makes our goods overseas either not marketable, or we have to lower our prices," Chandler said. "It's the lowering of prices that we generally do—that's what we did in the early Eighties. We even got to the point in Europe where we had an interval of time with no earnings. That's how far we had to go down in our price to keep the sales."

These are excruciating choices for managers: cut prices and lose profit margin, or lose market shares in the fierce global competition. The effects this time were not as severe as the earlier rolling recession that depressed manufacturing, but the costs were already visibly depressing Kodak's earnings. "For the year to date," Chandler said, "we're showing good volume growth around the world. By good volume growth, I'm saying I think it's between 7 and 9 percent this year. It was 9 percent last year, 11 percent the year before. But if you look at our revenues, they're not growing as fast. That difference is due to exchange-rate changes or the price changes we have been making as a result. It's several percentage points. On our revenue, several percentage points is big, big money, and it comes off the bottom line."

The bad news was reported in the company's quarterly statement: net earnings for the first half of 1989 were $487 million, a decline of 25 percent. These numbers excluded the one-time expenditures incurred through restructuring, which involved such cost-cutting measures as consolidating photofinishing and consumer photography units and taking associated write-offs of equipment, salaries, and goodwill. Those expenditures took earnings even lower. Other than that, business was terrific—sales were up 13 percent, even higher than Chandler had expected. Analysts at Wall Street brokerages, the same folks who had leaned on the Fed to raise interest rates and who had celebrated the rising dollar, now urged Colby Chandler to further cut internal costs to restore shareholder earnings. Chandler assured them that he would try, and he announced plans in August of 1989 to eliminate 4,500 jobs within the year and cut as much as 40 percent of the annual management payroll.

Across the entire economy, others benefited greatly from the economic dynamics that produced manufacturing's setback. The stronger dollar was especially profitable for banking and finance. An appreciated dollar reflects rising worldwide demand for what Wall Street has to sell—financial paper denominated in dollars. Consumers and retailers also benefited enormously; they enjoyed cheaper prices on imported goods. This trade-off of winners and losers, central to the consumption boom of the 1980s, was politically satisfying because most voters (and consumers) work in service sectors, not manufacturing or mining or agriculture, and they were not directly injured when those fields were battered.

But like so many other aspects of Reagan-era economics, this was a dreadful trade-off for America in the long term, another important instance of short-term gratification. The popular notion that the United States can simply evolve into a service economy, leaving factory production to other countries, is a distortion of the real nature of global trade. The overwhelming bulk of international trading volume is real goods, not intangible services. Worldwide trade in services during 1986 was only 19 percent of the trade in merchandise. For the United States, services accounted for only 29 percent of foreign trade in 1987, even though services represented nearly 51 percent of the U.S. gross national product. The reason for this is simple: most kinds of services, from health care to insurance, from the practice of law to education, are not readily transportable across national boundaries. Perhaps someday they will be, but that day is not soon.

The immediate implications for the United States are quite stark. The trade deficit, largely caused by the overvalued dollar's damage to manufacturing, has produced a huge national indebtedness to foreign creditors. Someday they must be paid back, and that will require the United States to accumulate trade *surpluses*. The only practical means to accomplish this rebalancing of international accounts is through the export of real goods—food, fiber, and manufactured products. This will be difficult in the best of circumstances. It will become virtually impossible if monetary policy keeps periodically hammering manufacturers with an appreciating dollar.

Kodak's corporate managers did not plan for the unpleasant turn of events in 1989, but then how could they? "We're very sophisticated—generally after the fact," the chairman explained. "When it comes to exchange rates, our current forecasting going into this year was about the same as it was in the early Eighties—that nobody knows whether the dollar is going up or down, so the forecast is flat."

That is what spooked Chandler. His company was flying blind again, into another storm, and it had still not recovered all that was lost in the last one. In terms of Kodak's own trade and currency exchanges, the dollar rose no less than 80 percent in the run-up that lasted from 1981 to 1985. Even Paul Volcker and other Federal Reserve governors admitted that the dollar had sailed too high during the 1980s and was devastating U.S. manufacturing. They regretted that outcome but insisted that it was an unfortunate side effect of their vigilant anti-inflation policy. Though it declined from 1985 to 1988, the dollar was still vastly overvalued when the Fed began its new campaign of tightening. "We never got back to zero on our curve," Chandler complained. "We never got back down to equilibrium, and now we're going back up again."

> **The money system effectively holds manufacturers like Kodak hostage to the perceptions of currency traders worldwide.**

The money system effectively holds manufacturers like Kodak hostage to the perceptions of currency traders worldwide, the banks and other financial institutions that play arbitrage games among competing currencies. Chandler is especially rankled that 90 percent of dollar-exchange transactions worldwide do not involve the trade of real goods and services but are for finance alone. As chairman of the President's Export Council, he is a leading participant in the competitiveness debate, but all of the talk about improving U.S. exports is rendered irrelevant by large dollar swings. "We ought to say, 'You're not going to trade our currency as a game,'" Chandler suggested. "Currency exchange is basically for commerce. There's something strange when it's as far out of line as it is now."

Besides cutting prices, multinational corporations have another option: they can close American factories and move production

9:33 PM, Memphis, Tennessee. Update sent from weather control.

Federal Express' weather forecasting system is the same one used by NASA.
Only they send men to the moon. And we send packages to your door.

9:40 PM, Somewhere over the Atlantic Ocean. Smooth flight to Europe.

The most advanced aircraft landing system in the industry,
Category III-A Avionics, enables Federal Express planes to land when others cannot.

abroad to foreign countries, where it will escape the artificial price disadvantage that monetary policy has created. Kodak's production structure limits its ability to use that ploy, but it tried in the early Eighties. "We shifted all we could into those overseas plants to run them at full tilt," Chandler said, "but that was not a very large coping strategy." Other corporations were more relentless about exporting jobs. A study by the Economic Policy Institute of Washington estimates that the U.S. trade deficits reflected a loss of 5.1 million jobs—60 percent of them in high-wage manufacturing. Millions of workers wound up in the lower-paying service jobs that the economy had created. The trade deficit that stifles American commerce is directly attributable to the stern monetary policy that dominated the 1980s and put U.S. producers at such a severe disadvantage. The country, like Kodak, has not yet recovered from that damage.

Corporations can, of course, try to hedge in the financial markets against currency changes, but that is a short-term tactic that really doesn't provide an escape from the long-term costs of currency shifts. As new contracts come up for negotiation, the buyers insist on the new prices that the escalating dollar has produced.

Colby Chandler, like most manufacturing executives, was a bit bashful about taking his complaints about the economy directly to the Fed. That's still considered impolite. Monetary policy drives their fortunes, but industrial managers are still mostly ignorant about the politics of money. "I had a stand-up conversation once at some reception in Washington with Paul Volcker when he was still chairman of the Fed, and I beat my gums on the subject," Chandler said. "But a stand-up conversation with Paul Volcker, for a guy who is 5 feet 8, is pretty uphill stuff." Volcker is 6 feet 7.

Alan Greenspan, the new Federal Reserve chairman, in the fall of 1988 provided the Senate banking committee with some stunning economic figures that, curiously, the press ignored. Greenspan's numbers described the bedrock reality of the 1980s and explained much about the turbulent era—the lopsided prosperity at the top, the periodic financial crises, the erosion of corporate balance sheets, and other unsettling developments. Yet both business and politics were reluctant to look directly at what these statistics revealed. The Fed chairman, of all people, was talking plainly about the true cost of money.

In response to written questions from the committee staff, Greenspan acknowledged that, yes, the real interest rates that prevailed

INFLATION-ADJUSTED INTEREST RATES

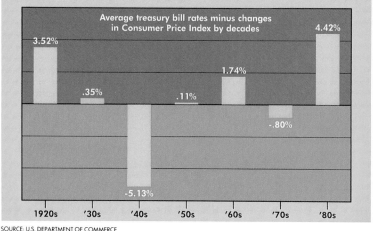

Average treasury bill rates minus changes in Consumer Price Index by decades

3.52%   .35%   -5.13%   .11%   1.74%   -.80%   4.42%

1920s   '30s   '40s   '50s   '60s   '70s   '80s

SOURCE: U.S. DEPARTMENT OF COMMERCE

throughout the decade were the highest of the 20th century. Greenspan's numbers, decade by decade, covered the bellwether rate on short-term treasury bills—the nominal interest rate minus the inflation rate, which gives the price of credit in real terms. Yet, as far as I could discover, the data were not published anywhere by general-interest newspapers or magazines. Academic economists did not schedule conferences to discuss the implications. Businessmen did not storm the capital, demanding relief from what these statistics disclosed.

The numbers revealed that the real cost of credit during the 1980s was more than 10 times the average rate of the preceding postwar years. For three decades, from 1950 to 1980, with inflation and without it, in the presence of both federal deficits and balanced budgets, the real interest rate fluctuated around an average of only 0.35 percent. That might seem small, but, historically, 0.35 percent represents a generous rate of real return on short-term T-bills. After all, lending one's money to the federal government for six months or a year is virtually free of risk. In the 1980s, lenders received a real return of 4.42 percent on the same transaction.

Similar lopsided rewards went to all creditors, whether they were lending money to consumers buying houses or to corporations investing in new productive capacity. The extraordinary level of real interest represented a fundamental shift in how economic returns would be distributed throughout the society—between lenders and borrowers, between capital owners and entrepreneurial enterprise, between the haves and the have-nots. The inflated rates meant that a vastly larger share of national income was shifted to the top of society, the holders of wealth and the institutions that stored it. This helps explain many of the social pathologies that became so evident—the degradation of homeless families and the gilded consumption binges of newly rich financiers, the continuing waves of failed debtors and the accompanying crises for financial institutions. The decade-by-decade numbers disclosed that the bloated interest rates of the 1980s were rivaled during only one other period in this century—the Roaring Twenties, when similarly distorted social values were in full play.

In explanatory remarks, Greenspan repeated the syllogism that his predecessor, Paul Volcker, had successfully promoted throughout the decade. The central bank and its foreign counterparts were not to blame. The high real rates were simply a function of the huge federal deficits and low savings rates that unfolded in the Reagan years, a problem of too many borrowers competing for scarce capital. Almost everyone, from corporate CEOs like Kodak's Colby Chandler to the senators and representatives who argued endlessly over reducing the deficits, accepted this easy explanation. The Fed blamed the politicians and absolved itself. In the giddy atmosphere of the Reagan years, most people thought that surely the conservative central bank had it right.

This widespread faith that the federal deficits were the source of all distress was not undermined in the least by the abundance of contradictory facts. The extraordinary rise of real interest rates, for instance, did not begin with the huge federal deficits of the Reagan era. It started in 1981, when the Federal Reserve applied heavy brakes to the American economy. The real rates, furthermore, did not subside after Congress made substantial reductions in the deficits. The federal deficit shrank by one-third in 1987, yet real interest rates rose smartly and continued upward the following year. The explanation was not a secret: the Federal Reserve was tightening money.

Greenspan's numbers show that during the 1940s, when the federal government borrowed on a gargantuan scale for World War II, real interest rates were negative. The Fed, in those years, kept nominal long-term rates at a steady, stable 2 percent, and federal deficits as a percentage of the gross national product then dwarfed the deficits of the Eighties. Indeed, the current federal deficits may have been directly aggravated by the Fed's regime of tight monetary policy, because the high real rates pushed up the cost of federal borrowing. The high rates also forced consumers and businesses to borrow more to keep up the payments and stave off default.

For many of the same reasons, the rate of domestic savings throughout the 1980s was low—the opposite of what conservative theory had predicted when Reagan's supply-side cuts were enacted. As John Maynard Keynes had explained 50 years earlier, personal savings accumulate rapidly only in a fast-growing economy. When wage earners enjoy rising incomes, they can set aside more and more as savings.

Despite congratulatory propaganda, the economy of the 1980s was not robust in this context. Real wages declined. The rate of growth was slower than during the decade before. Unemployment had declined by 1989 to about 5 percent, but only after five years of relatively high unemployment, in which the unemployed exhausted their savings merely to survive. Those at the top, with accumulated capital, were paid an extraordinary premium to lend their wealth to those struggling beneath them. The net consequence for the nation was a low savings rate.

When borrowers are forced to pay an exorbitant share of their incomes to the lenders, their own wherewithal is gradually devoured in servicing the debts.

The Fed's strategy, which Volcker consistently obscured with his opaque public statements, would not have been possible if the financial system had not been deregulated first. Deregulation took the limit off interest rates, and the Federal Reserve pushed rates to new heights. But, in fairness to the Fed governors, deregulation also forced them into a corner.

By repealing the old interest-rate ceilings, Congress was removing important circuit breakers that the central bank depended on to control the economy. In the past, when the Fed nudged rates high enough to bump against the legal ceilings, lending dried up, and that slowed down economic activity. Without the credit controls, the Fed felt it had no choice but to push the cost of credit higher and higher. It had to accept the collateral costs like the soaring dollar that decimated U.S. manufacturing and the continuing waves of bankruptcies. When borrowers are forced to pay an exorbitant share of their incomes to the lenders, their own wherewithal is gradually devoured in servicing the debts. Eventually, they can no longer borrow at all. The real rates, in other words, sap economic energy and, one way or another, produce the continuing defaults and recurring breakdowns in the financial system. Even sophisticated people often do not grasp the crucial point that the principal beneficiaries of the old system of regulated credit were not just families borrowing to consume, but businesses borrowing to produce and sell. Business directly suffered the deleterious effects of the new order. The gross costs of the unprecedented real interest rates imposed by the Federal Reserve were paid by American industry—especially by those manufacturers who were struggling to restructure and modernize. Every corporate budget reflected a higher operating cost, just as the federal government's budget did. Corporations saddled with takeover debt paid an even larger premium.

The real rates meant a higher cost of capital for American corporations, particularly when compared with competitors in Asia or Europe. Various studies have calculated that corporate borrowers in the U.S. paid effective rates on capital in the mid-1980s that were three to seven percentage points higher than what companies paid in Japan. The government, urging U.S. industry to modernize, simultaneously discouraged investment by keeping the price too high. As long as this differential remains, there is no way that American companies can expect to keep up in the competitiveness contest.

Colby Chandler worries about that too. As a director of Citicorp, he has brought up the question at board meetings, but the bankers scoff at the problem. "They think the real interest rates are okay," Chandler said. "I've watched this real interest rate go up to 4 percent, and of course higher at times, and I talk about bringing it back down. But I think there is a general mood that this current real interest rate is the new norm. Financial institutions in general have built it into a cost structure which assumes it as normal."

What happened in the 1980s was not normal. But the damaging effects will continue to accumulate, with occasional costly crises, as long as everyone accepts the bankers'—and the Federal Reserve's—judgment on these matters.

"It sure doesn't feel like a soft landing in Detroit," the chief economist at Prudential-Bache Securities, Edward Yardeni, advised the firm's clients. The big three auto companies had just reduced midsummer 1989 production schedules to an annual rate of five million cars—their lowest output since the trough of the 1982 recession. Cars make up 16 percent of durable goods in the U.S., and in the past, when the housing and auto sectors slid into recession, the rest of the economy followed. Yardeni, like most Wall Street economists, did not expect this to happen now. The Fed would prevent it, he said, by easing interest rates in a timely fashion.

The auto executives in Detroit had read all of the confident forecasts but were no longer so sure that they could believe them. As the Fed tightened, the companies launched another blitz of interest-rate incentives to prop up sales, but this time the deep discounts did not produce much. "We've now got a consumer conditioned to rebates—concessionary pricing—and it's like dope," said Robert Liberatore, Chrysler's executive director of public policy and legislative affairs. "Once they've gotten used to it, we can't stop it."

Auto sales kept falling, just like home sales and retail sales. This should not have surprised anyone, given what the Fed had done to interest rates. The economy was following the classic path to recession, and only a strong reversal by the Federal Reserve might avert the classic consequences: rising unemployment and bankruptcies. Even if an economywide contraction was avoided, the rolling recession that had so damaged manufacturing in the mid-1980s had now rolled back to Detroit.

"The way the Fed slows down the economy is to raise interest rates, and it hits housing, autos, and other interest-sensitive sectors," complained Donald P. Hilty, the corporate economist at Chrysler. "We wonder: Is this the only way to cool down the economy? Why does the Fed have to hit housing and manufacturing? It's a meat-ax approach when we need a scalpel. When we say that, the Fed comes back and says, 'We know it's a meat ax, but that's all we've got.'"

UPSIDE DOWN CAR

Paying off five-year loans on their old cars has forced many consumers out of the market for new cars.

This time, the auto companies bumped into new impediments to sales that were direct legacies of the high real interest rates that had prevailed throughout the decade. It wasn't the interest rate on new cars that inhibited many potential buyers; it was the debt they were still stuck with on their old cars. To get around the high interest rates earlier in the decade, car loans were often stretched out to 60 months or even longer. The trouble was that after making payments for three or four years, the owner discovered that his money had gone mostly for interest payments and he had accumulated little or no equity. The car was wearing out, and he would have liked to buy a new one, but couldn't because trading in the old car wouldn't give him enough to make a decent down payment. So he kept driving the old car, and Detroit lost another sale.

The auto industry calls these people upside-down car owners and worries about the implications because their number seems to be growing. "We're trying to understand what drives this," Hilty said. "Is this a ceiling on auto-industry growth?" In fact, upside-down car owners are much like upside-down homeowners: the young families who take on mortgages they can't afford, and who eventually decide to walk away from the payments and their homes.

The holders of variable-rate mortgages and equity-line loans felt the squeeze of rising payments directly in their disposable incomes. "We figure about 25 percent of the mortgages are now variable

8:53 AM, Near San Francisco Bay. Morning deliveries.

Federal Express delivers coast-to-coast
by 10:30 in the morning.

8:53 AM, Along Boston Harbor. Morning deliveries.

Federal Express controls your shipment throughout its entire journey.
We pick it up. We sort it. We fly it. And we deliver it.

rates," Hilty said. "For those people, the monthly payments would go up as much as $250 and that would preclude them from buying a car. It takes away their disposable income and knocks them out of the market."

Even if the Fed managed to avert a recession, its policy was putting the American auto industry into a deep hole, further weakening it for competition with foreign producers. A new round was playing out within the United States as the Japanese companies opened more plants and began more domestic production. The struggle for market shares was intensifying, and some auto-assembly plants were sure to be closed. U.S. auto production was operating at only about 75 percent of capacity, Robert Liberatore said, and the industry expected anywhere from five to 10 major factories to be rendered obsolete over the next several years.

In the context of this struggle, the Federal Reserve had handed the Japanese companies a tremendous advantage by allowing the dollar to rise again by 15 or 20 percent. "It's going to allow the Japanese to hold their prices down and increase their market share, just because of the 20 percent jump in the dollar," Liberatore explained. Hilty added: "The Japanese have gotten the equivalent of about a 20 percent price increase, and it's a windfall for them."

The Chrysler economist sounded increasingly gloomy about the long-run prospects. "We're in really a tragic period," Hilty said. "The more interest rates increase, the more we cut costs and add incentives to keep sales figures propped up. The better we look, the more the Fed says, 'Let's tighten the screws more.'"

Hilty said that Chrysler's blunt chairman, Lee Iacocca, had also berated the system: "Historians will look back someday on how we tried to cure inflation, and they will think it is as silly as bloodletting."

Bloodletting was an apt metaphor. Especially in the auto industry and other manufacturing fields, that was what the Fed's suppression of demand resembled. In autos, for instance, the worldwide demand for cars in the late 1980s was about 35 million a year, but the world's capacity to make cars is about 45 million a year. That gap describes a global economic dilemma—insufficient demand for goods and excessive capacity to produce them. The glut of supply covers everything from computers to finished steel to grain, and this reality frames the contest among trading nations. Both politicians and business executives struggle to answer the question, Whose factories are going to be closed?

The Federal Reserve's cure for domestic price inflation seems to be a strategy to make the global economic problem even worse, to

"Historians will look back someday on how we tried to cure inflation, and they will think it is as silly as bloodletting."

bleed a little more demand out of the American economy and see if that eventually makes the patient well.

When the Federal Reserve finally relented in the spring of 1989 and slowly began lowering interest rates, some people feared that it might already be too late. The downshift in economic activity was confirmed almost daily in the business news, and Chairman Greenspan's public remarks abruptly took on a defensive tone. The Federal Reserve, he began to emphasize, was not infallible. Should a recession develop, it would be a mistake, not a deliberate policy choice. "What we seek to avoid," Greenspan promised, "is an unnecessary and destructive recession."

These words were not likely to comfort those who would absorb the consequences of a Fed mistake. Even if recession was avoided, the depressing effects of the Fed's tightening campaign were already feeding through the economy and producing a new collection of losers. A soft landing would put another half-million or so people out of work and spread the debtor defaults and bankruptcies in new directions.

Greenspan himself was known to worry about what might happen if a recession swiftly unraveled into something worse—a general cascade of defaulting debtors. In particular, the overleveraged corporations made the economy quite fragile. If recession took hold, debt-ridden companies would have to scramble to cut costs quickly in order to keep up with their interest payments. That would require swiftly closing the factories and pushing unemployment up. Once launched, the ripple effect might move faster than the federal regulators.

"I guess I'm banking on Greenspan," said Chrysler's Donald Hilty. "I don't think in his heart of hearts he wants a recession. The Fed's tools are very crude, and he's pretty cocky about his fine-tuning ability, but I think that as soon as he can get away with it, he's going to push on the accelerator."

Robert J. Barbera, chief economist at Shearson Lehman Hutton, congratulated the central bank on its skillful steering and assured clients in mid-1989 that a recession was not in the cards. Nevertheless, Barbera warned:

"U.S. financial system risk will be tested over the next six months. The successful Fed-engineered U.S. economic downshift has capped revenue streams at many companies saddled with large debts. Bankruptcies are bound to rise; nonperforming loans will surprise bankers; and a few heavily leveraged companies may fail.... These events, though devastating for those directly involved, will not seriously threaten the U.S. financial system."

The question Wall Street analysts usually ducked was whether any of this pain and failure was really necessary. The general assumption was that the Federal Reserve had done the right thing by reacting to the alarms of incipient runaway inflation and cooling down the economy in a timely manner. The alarms had not originated with consumers but had come from Wall Street markets. In hindsight, the facts simply did not support Wall Street's inflation anxieties.

The inflation rate bounces up and down month to month for many complicated reasons, but over time there was simply no evidence that a general price run-up was rippling across the economy, despite the claims of Wall Street experts. By July of 1989, the Consumer Price Index was rising at a tepid pace of 0.2 percent per month, an inflation rate that would be less than 3 percent per year. In fact, if one excluded the impact of energy and food, consumer prices declined slightly in the first half of 1989.

Likewise, the claim that wages were about to break out of control was simply false. Employee wages, salaries, and benefits had risen over the prior 12 months by 4.5 percent—exactly the same increase as in the previous period. While workers in some selected areas were enjoying real gains, labor as a whole was still losing ground. Pay raises were not keeping up with the general rise of prices. Wages in real terms were still falling, as they had throughout the decade.

In fact, the inflation alarms that became the conventional wisdom and drove the central bank to depress the entire economy were concocted out of peculiar events, not out of a general trend. The summer drought of 1988 produced shortfalls in agricultural output, which naturally led to a surge in commodity prices. Simultaneously, OPEC (Organization of Petroleum Exporting Countries) managed to discipline excess production enough to push oil prices up from the recessionary level of $13 a barrel to about $20 a barrel. Both of those factors fed through the American economy at once and produced a temporary illusion of generally escalating prices.

The drought's impact on food prices was, of course, utterly unavoidable. The increase in oil prices was actually healthy for America because higher prices helped ease the recession and financial disorders in the Southwest and stimulated conservation by consumers. By the spring of 1989, the one-time impact from both of these events had already dissipated, and commodity prices were falling again. Meanwhile, the Federal Reserve was hammering the entire American economy, trying to slow it down.

As this episode suggests, the money system works in a less-than-rational way. It does not make sense, for instance, to suppress the whole U.S. economy because a drought wiped out the Midwest corn crop, or because the oil nations regained, at least temporarily, a handle on oil prices. Above all, smashing American manufacturing and its workers and owners is senseless when other sectors of the economy are producing the price inflation. It *is* a meat-ax approach. It *is* as senseless as bloodletting.

The basic contradictions are visible to anyone who takes the trouble to look closely at price inflation. Manufacturing, for instance, did not produce the inflation rate of 3 to 4 percent that persisted through much of the 1980s. Service industries, from medical care to finance, drove inflation up. Statistics show this clearly: service sectors consistently inflated their prices every year by 5 to 7 percent and sometimes more, while the goods-producing industries—and their supposedly powerful unions—achieved price increases at a rate below the national average.

If discipline is required to maintain price stability, wouldn't punishing the offenders be more rational? The Fed's disciplinary system works in the opposite manner: it punishes the innocent. Service sectors generally escape the brunt of higher interest rates for several reasons: they do not have to carry large inventories of goods and materials; their sales are usually not dependent on credit; and most of them do not have to compete in the global market where currency changes can arbitrarily undercut their profits. For all of those reasons, manufacturing takes it in the neck. The full burden of the Fed's punishment falls on the producers of real goods—from copper miners in Arizona to wheat farmers in Kansas to Eastman Kodak in Rochester, New York—and they pay the penalty for the excesses of others.

This is unjust. And blindly destructive. In the long run, it is also terrible economics. What the money system inadvertently accomplishes by applying the brakes through general interest rates is accelerating the shrinkage of real-goods sectors that are the vital core of the American economy. Given the U.S. trade deficit and the country's mounting debt obligations to foreign creditors, government policy ought to be fostering the opposite—the growth of U.S. manufacturing—because ultimately those debts will have to be paid. The only reliable way to pay them is through trading more real goods to other countries. The alternative is less pleasant: selling off

Smashing American manufacturing and its workers and owners is senseless when other sectors of the economy are producing the price inflation.

more and more U.S. assets to the foreign creditors and accepting a lower standard of living in America.

The conservative status quo, both at the Federal Reserve and elsewhere, has good reason not to face these gross contradictions that blanket the government's regulation of money and the financial system. That would require authorities to face the hard political task of developing quite different methods and objectives. They would have to invent other ways, more selective and less brutal than the current ones, to manipulate the economy. New rules would have to be written on the behavior of banking and finance and on the guarantees with which the government provides them.

These are all daunting challenges, fraught with difficult politics, but not impossible to master if the politicians will face them honestly. Smugness is still in the saddle, however. The conservative order, having won so many elections, is not in the least willing to face its failures. The political leadership of both parties is reluctant to challenge the considerable power of the vested financial interests. Citizens, not having suffered calamity, do not yet see their own grave exposure.

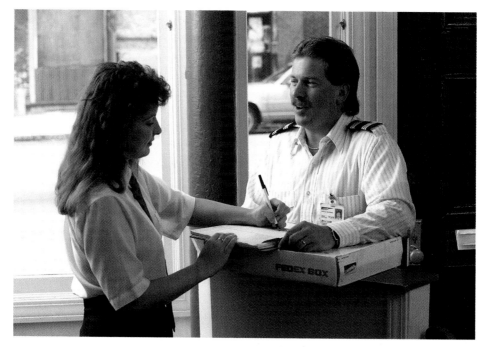

9:17 AM, McKay, Idaho. International package is delivered.

Federal Express helps expedite the timely delivery of international shipments by closely working with customs officials worldwide.

FAREWELL
TO
LAISSEZ-
FAIRE

CHAPTER
6

The conservative order has been permissive on a reckless scale and fatalistic about the consequences. The government, conservatives argue, can do nothing except let the marketplace sort things out. The free run of markets will ultimately generate new economic activity and new wealth—with only occasional wreckage—and a rough sense of order and justice will emerge. In the long run, we will all be better off. This stout-hearted sentiment is as ancient as capitalism, and it led to John Maynard Keynes's famous rejoinder: In the long run, we are all dead.

The trouble with the laissez-faire creed in its contemporary version is that it is only a sentiment, not a serious idea. The last thing that American banking and financial markets would tolerate now would be for government to withdraw from their territory and leave them alone to face the brutal consequences of genuine freedom. They desperately need government to protect them from the harsh realities of the marketplace. The users of credit are subjected to the bracing discipline of failure. The dispensers of credit are shielded from market forces by their government. This arrangement is so illogical, not to mention unjust, that it cannot endure. And it won't.

The reregulation of banking and finance is not only inevitable but already fitfully under way. Most people do not yet grasp this fact, and given the prevailing conservative ethos, the regulators are not eager to announce it. While banks and other financial firms are still tugging and pulling at the law, searching for new loopholes, the tide has already turned in practical political terms, though not yet in ideological fashion. Awkward necessity has forced the government to ignore sentimental laissez-faire and begin, at least haphazardly, to reconstruct some controls over private finance.

The savings and loan bailout legislation represents one attempt to restore legal discipline, but the new rules are grossly inadequate. The largest commercial banks, likewise, have belatedly been required to meet higher capital standards, but the regulators still lack adequate tools to enforce restraint. These measures and others will raise the cost of indulging in reckless behavior for bankers and their stockholders, but the new regulations do not confront fundamental flaws in the status quo.

A much more significant step toward sensible reregulation—mostly unknown outside banking circles—was initiated without fanfare by the major central banks of the industrial world. Together, the Federal Reserve and its counterparts in Japan, Britain, France, Germany, Italy, and six other industrialized countries agreed to impose, starting in 1992, a new system of internationally coordinated capital requirements on the largest commercial banks, geared specifically to the level of risk reflected in each bank's loan portfolio. This agreement was reached in Basel, Switzerland, in July of 1988, after several years of negotiation, prompted mainly by U.S. regulators traumatized by the various banking crises of the 1980s.

After the enormity of third-world debt began surfacing in 1982, the Federal Reserve realized that it had not done much to head off dangerously excessive levels of debt at the largest money-center banks. The new measures were intended to give the Fed a better handle on the lending behavior of those banks, particularly the banks' so-called off-balance-sheet obligations, such as letters of credit, that were beyond the reach of old regulatory measures. U.S. banks went along with the proposal and even encouraged it. They hoped that tougher capital rules, if applied internationally, might reduce the competitive edge enjoyed by their larger rivals in Japan and elsewhere.

At least in theory, the new mechanism, known as risk-based capital ratios, would give regulators a potent tool for steering banks away from certain kinds of lending that appear dangerous. If banks became overexposed in their loan commitments to, say, Latin American nations or junk-bond takeover deals, regulators could raise the risk assessment on these types of loans and thus compel the banks to post more capital behind them. The net effect would be to reduce the banks' profit margin on such lending—giving a "haircut" to the banks' interest-rate spread, as bankers say. That cost restraint, if forcefully applied, would presumably discourage the bankers from plunging further into the swamp. While the theory is untested, this new regulation may eventually provide the structure on which political reformers can build more substantial controls—if the political system is ever willing to face the dangers that regulators already recognize.

In the meantime, a low-volume technical debate is already under way among academics, government regulators, and financial-industry experts over exactly how the government might stabilize the financial system. They have reached a rough consensus that new government powers are needed to restore balance and reduce the risk of larger calamities. Gerald Corrigan, president of the New York Fed, for instance, has sketched plausible outlines for reregulation that would extend government supervision to the competing financial players beyond the commercial banks. Henry Kaufman, the former chief economist at Salomon Brothers, has argued for a new federal board of financial overseers with extraordinary powers to reconcile conflicting practices in different financial arenas. A study commissioned by the Brookings Institution has recommended a new fail-safe system for troubled banks: a rule would compel federal regulators to seize control of a distressed bank when its capital base declined below a certain level—that is, long before the bank was faced with failure.

These reform proposals embody some astute ideas and some impossible ones, but the suggestions all suffer from the same handicap: narrow vision. The debate about financial reregulation is confined to insiders, who are focusing on the internal mechanics of bank operations and on regulatory control to ensure soundness. The bankers will naturally do whatever they can politically to shape the outcome of the reregulation debate in their own favor.

No one has yet asked the larger economic and social questions that might provoke a larger political debate about the money system—a debate in which everyone else would be able to recognize his or her own stake in the subject. Corporate managers have a powerful stake in the regulatory debate; so do homebuilders, farmers, labor leaders, consumers, and taxpayers. The regulation of money reaches deeply

Corporate managers have a powerful stake in the regulatory debate; so do homebuilders, farmers, labor leaders, consumers, and taxpayers.

into all their lives and economic well-being. The governing system, like it or not, has the capacity to alter, sometimes quite drastically, the fortunes of every economic interest in the nation, and that governing system is now malfunctioning.

Nostalgia for free-market solutions endures despite the vivid evidence that modern economies, including America's, depend in complicated ways on government management and intervention, especially in crises. Still, the hope persists. Why can't the government simply allow the big banks to fail? Why not withdraw, at least partially, the federal safety net of deposit insurance and other guarantees so that both depositors and stockholders will be subject to the market discipline of loss? Learned essays promoting this approach are published regularly in conservative quarterlies and *The Wall Street Journal*. The free-market idea is alluring in theory: give the banks and their customers a taste of bad medicine, and they will soon behave themselves. Alas, the theory falls apart when introduced to the realities of both finance and politics.

If political leaders, for instance, ever decide to remove, even fractionally, the blanket protection of federal deposit insurance, they had better make the announcement late at night when the banks are closed. The next morning the lines would form in bank lobbies as confused and anxious depositors played it safe by withdrawing their money—not from all banks, but from lots of them, the ones believed to be in trouble. The conservative theorists seem unaware of the deep public nervousness that already exists about financial institutions, anxiety fed regularly by reading the newspapers.

Free-market theory assumes that every participant will seek the best available information and that the collective decisions of markets will therefore be rational. But in the real world, average depositors are not bank analysts. As a practical matter, they have no means of their own for checking out a bank's soundness. So typically they will react to rumors, true or false, and flee at the first hint of danger, even if the danger is the possibility that they might lose, say, 15 percent of their money by leaving it in the wrong bank. Eliminating this sort of wildfire fear from the banking system was the original purpose of 100 percent federal deposit insurance back in 1933, and on the whole, it worked. Bank runs by the general public ceased. Most politicians will not be eager to test laissez-faire propositions that might bring back this destructive phenomenon.

The crucial problem, in any case, involves not the small depositors but the largest ones—the institutional investors, other banks, local governments, pension funds, whoever invests billions in jumbo CDs at commercial banks and S&Ls. Modern bank runs are initiated electronically and with dizzying speed whenever these big investors pick up a hint of serious trouble. They simply move their money elsewhere and, in extreme cases, the bank is doomed. That's when federal regulators step in with their extraordinary assurances to the largest depositors. In theory, these folks are not covered by federal insurance, but in practice, federal regulators need to reassure them too or face the possibility of a cascading panic that ripples across the money market and threatens other major banks with similar difficulties.

The Federal Reserve chairman and other regulators might, for instance, have accepted the collapse of the Continental Illinois Bank in 1984 and even the collateral costs of a hundred or so small banks that would have failed with it. What they could not face was the risk that the ensuing turmoil in the money market—investors seeking safe haven in the storm—might also pull down several other money-center banks. Bank of America, Chase Manhattan, Chemical, Manufacturers Hanover Trust—all of these and others were vulnerable to the same sort of panic. How much destruction could the financial system stand in the name of disciplining the players? The Federal Reserve, created back in 1913 to prevent this sort of calamity, is not willing to find out. Propping up Continental and the other banks deemed too big to fail is done in the name of defending the system itself.

Whether the regulators' case-by-case judgment is right or wrong is beside the point. The underlying reality is that neither political nor financial leaders are willing to risk a larger breakdown of finance. That applies far beyond banks to the largest brokerages and government-guaranteed securities corporations and many others. When Bache Group, now Prudential-Bache Securities, was in deep trouble in the early 1980s, executives did not call Milton Friedman for advice. They called Paul Volcker for help.

The free-market nostalgists do not honestly face these questions, of course, because the case for genuine laissez-faire is more a wish than an argument—a deeply felt yearning to return to "normal times." For the most visionary conservatives, this would entail going back as far as 1913 and dismantling the historic compromise that banking made with politics when the Federal Reserve was created to protect the soundness of the system. Others would settle for going back to 1932.

A return to genuine laissez-faire is improbable, above all because these are not normal times. The recurring conditions of financial disorder are not temporary aberrations but flow from the system itself. The extraordinary debt accumulation alone does not lead to continuing episodes of financial crisis; the extraordinary level of interest rates collected on that debt also contribute. The inadequate regulation of financial institutions alone does not cause the problem; the inadequate system of managing the economy through monetary policy is also responsible. All of these factors interact in debilitating ways. Genuine reform will require not simply fixing one dimension of the problem but gaining the political courage to address the whole.

External limits are needed to prevent both lenders and borrowers from being consumed by self-destructive transactions.

The essential challenge of reform will be to invent a new regulatory system for money and credit—a new governing arrangement of safety valves and circuit breakers—that restores both stability and equity. Such a system would empower the Federal Reserve to manage the economy in a way that prevents runaway price inflation without forcing interest rates to the level that produces continuing financial disorders. Free-market illusions must be put aside, and the ancient economic truth embedded in the biblical concept of usury must be accepted instead. External limits are needed to prevent both lenders and borrowers from being consumed by self-destructive transactions. The goal of financial reform should be to restore the braking powers that were implicit in the old regulatory system's interest-rate ceilings, while avoiding the crude rigidities and inequities that eventually doomed that system.

Attaining this goal would require the establishment of sophisticated regulatory mechanisms across many fronts. The politics of implementing such a system would be especially daunting, since the status quo satisfies so many powerful interests. I offer my own brief sketch of how a reformed system might work, not with any illusion that these ideas are likely to be accepted soon by conventional opinion, but with considerable confidence that sooner or later the debate will turn in this direction.

The easiest starting point for reform would be to elaborate on those risk-based capital ratios recently adopted by the central banks. With additional force and flexibility, those controls could be employed as discreet levers on the credit-creating process simply by raising banks' lending costs when authorities see the danger of inflationary run-ups. This would have the advantage of choking off new lending at its source without requiring the Fed to push interest rates to extraordinary levels. The braking effect could either be applied generally across the economy or targeted at particular sectors where inflationary bubbles were developing.

Such a system would directly acknowledge what the experience of the 1980s has taught: higher interest rates don't dampen lending in the way previously assumed. The Fed held real interest rates at outlandish levels, trying to restrain debt creation, but debt of all kinds mushroomed anyway. Indeed, many borrowers were compelled by the higher rates to go even deeper into debt to stay alive. Both corporations and consumers will keep borrowing when they are threatened by bankruptcy, regardless of how imprudent it may seem. As long as both bankers and borrowers are willing, the bubble gets larger and larger, until it is pricked by default. The new system would be designed to restrain *both* sides of the credit transaction well before they reach such extremes.

The net result could be an effective but flexible way of producing limits on interest rates. The governors of monetary policy would not have to revive Regulation Q with its rigid ceilings, but they could operate with well-understood guidelines on the level of real interest rates. As inflation rose, rates also would be allowed to ride up to maintain a real return for investors—but so would the internal cost pressures on banks to curb lending.

Among other benefits, this approach might allow government to focus restraint on the right culprits and avoid punishing the wrong victims, to see beyond the misleading averages and look at what is actually happening to prices. Once a general inflationary binge is under way, that sort of selective restraint is impossible. But before it reaches that stage, the Fed could use its power over bank-loan portfolios to apply the brakes early in sectors where credit creation is clearly inflationary. If a speculative bubble were to develop in housing or agriculture, the Fed could squeeze housing or agriculture. It wouldn't have to punish other interest-sensitive sectors like manufacturing because something else is out of control.

The orthodox objection to this sort of approach is that such controls would put the federal government in the business of credit allocation, diverting the supply of credit toward some users and away from others. But the government is already in that business in a large way, with both its vast federal credit programs of subsidy and guarantee and with the Federal Reserve's manipulation of interest rates. The Fed already rations credit, but it allocates with high rates that force the weaker and smaller customers out of the market. That system of control favors the largest, most wealthy players, and they naturally prefer to keep it that way for as long as possible.

The Fed's new risk-based capital-ratio rules applied to bank-loan portfolios also effectively allocate credit to certain users. By assigning different risk ratios to different categories of lending, the Fed has already implicitly accepted the role of pushing banks toward some customers and away from others. Its ability to do that for broad public purposes needs to be developed further. Finally, the regulators' deep interventions on behalf of struggling financial institutions also constitute a perverse form of credit allocation—choosing winners and losers. In short, it's a bit late in the day for federal regulators to claim aloofness or for the bankers to assert their right to privacy.

Another objection to rehabilitating credit controls focuses on the global financial system. America, conservatives say, cannot reregulate the financial system because finance is now international. This was the argument originally advanced for deregulation and was always grossly exaggerated. While the United States was repealing its governing standards for the financial system, other industrial nations, such as Japan, were keeping most of theirs. Although Japan has deregulated parts of its financial markets, it still operates what is basically an administered credit system. This fact does not seem to have prevented Japan from participating fully in global finance or from acquiring a major foothold in the U.S. system.

In any case, the new international rules negotiated by the leading central banks, including the Fed, specifically render the objection moot. The risk-based capital-ratio rules allow each individual nation to adopt its own controls for domestic finance. Indeed, the Federal Reserve initially proposed risk standards for U.S. banks that would have been more punitive to housing than the standards in the other nations. It backed off only because of political objections at home.

Another fundamental premise of reform would make the governing system more rational by acknowledging the obvious: the powerful levers over credit and the economy are not located just at the Fed but are spread across the federal government. There is a bizarre pretense that fiscal policy and monetary policy can be independently managed. That fiction allowed, even encouraged, the destructive conflict between tight money and huge deficits in the 1980s.

The federal government's own vast credit programs are operated as though the Federal Reserve doesn't even exist. When the central bank tries to restrain inflation, the rest of government blithely pumps out billions of dollars in new loans and loan guarantees as though its borrowers were somehow exempt from the forces of high interest rates and a depressed economy. Lots of farmers with government loans found out differently in the 1980s.

The least one might reasonably expect from Washington is that its various centers of power try to pull in the same direction. If one lever of power is in the process of forcing an economic slowdown, the other levers should not be stimulating the opposite. A coordinated system would require abandoning the notion of an independent Federal Reserve. The government would have to become more systematic—and more candid—about how it determines the course of the economy.

Once the government reformed its methods of regulating the economy, it would also be better equipped to prevent the kind of financial crises and failures of the 1980s. There will always be crooked bankers, of course, just as there will always be foolish borrowers, but both could be directly inhibited from the worst forms of folly and error if regulators had the powers that new controls could provide. If the new system did not require extraordinary levels of real interest rates, there would be far fewer casualties in banking—and certainly fewer innocent ones.

The least one might reasonably expect from Washington is that its various centers of power try to pull in the same direction.

Regulatory concerns involving turf—the political battle that energizes commercial banks and their competitors—are the hardest to tackle. Reregulation, as Gerald Corrigan and others have suggested, must guarantee that commercial banks dwell in a secure and profitable realm so they can fill their traditional role of credit watchdog without being driven to irresponsible risk-taking. As that implies, banks are special institutions in the economy, and they must be protected as well as regulated.

The scope of regulation should be broadened to cover all of those other financial players that have been riding free on implicit government protection, from the major Wall Street brokerages to the new hybrid all-service financial firms. One of the principal reasons the old regulatory system broke down was that it did not attempt to impose comparable rules of restraint on financial institutions, such as money-market funds, that compete with commercial banks and savings and loans. As the unregulated firms picked off both depositors and loan customers, the effectiveness of Regulation Q was gradually eviscerated. The pressure to free the banks from the legal limits grew irresistibly strong. Nothing proposed here is likely to work if political reformers look narrowly at commercial banks and S&Ls and ignore the rest.

The largest commercial banks, in my judgment, will have to be regarded in the future as public utilities, shielded by law in some

As American banking becomes much more concentrated at the top, it will gain the political power to establish priorities for communities and regions, even for the nation.

ways and even provided a guaranteed return, but also obligated to serve broader public purposes. That role would be a partial solution to the problem of banks that are now deemed too big to fail. An additional incentive would be to declare that in the event of the failure of one of these very large banks, the institution would become a public bank in the full sense. It would be owned and operated to fulfill regional or national objectives, such as industrial redevelopment, rather than solely to achieve maximum profit. This rule, I think, would send a powerful cautionary message to bankers everywhere.

These notions may sound a bit visionary at this moment of history, but I expect that the future will make them seem more plausible. As American banking becomes much more concentrated in the next few years, especially at the top, the need for fundamental redefinition should become evident. Banking power involves much more than economics. Banking is political power as well. It is the power to establish priorities for communities and regions, even for the nation. As these powers are consolidated in a smaller and smaller number of huge national banking organizations, the public may at last begin to grasp that the arcane subject of money regulation has direct social consequences for everyone.

An even larger challenge awaits the political system down the road: rehabilitating the social contract. That is another task that the governing elites do not yet wish to face, but certain aspects are already painfully visible. The changed financial system has been intimately involved in the dismantling of the old promises articulated as the American dream. The restoration of those old social commitments will also depend greatly on finance and banking. The housing crisis, for instance, could be resolved directly and efficiently if the financial system were required to pool sufficient capital to provide below-market mortgage rates for first-time home-buyers and low-income housing construction. The government could, in effect, require owners of wealth and the financial institutions to accept a modest social burden in exchange for the protections that government provides them. That would mean a small, barely noticeable nick in their potential return, yet it would create the market demand for new housing that is necessary to solve this crisis.

In similar terms, if the political community ever settled on clear goals for rebuilding American industry, the financial system and its investors could be required to share the burden of the established national priorities, just as they do in other countries, such as Japan. That burden would mean accepting a lower rate of return in the short term in the interest of fulfilling long-term economic goals. Other societies have demonstrated that when such long-range goals are fulfilled, everyone profits in the end, especially the wealthy.

But who would decide on these priorities? Who would determine the broad public objectives that the banking system and everyone else must help meet? In a democracy, the political system—the elected governors and representatives—is supposed to perform that function. Cynics will contend that the debate would quickly founder in the narrow interest-group politics of contemporary Washington. This may be the strongest argument one could make against most of my suggestions: that the American political system, in its present atrophied state, may have lost its capacity to mediate such difficult matters, to set national priorities and pursue them in a manner that almost everyone would accept.

To acknowledge the relevance of this argument does not, however, require one to succumb to permanent cynicism. American democracy, through its low periods and high points, has retained a stubborn capacity to self-correct, however belatedly. Eras of real reform are rare, and they usually come only after enough people have become sufficiently angry to get themselves educated and engaged. Political tides shift and new ideas suddenly become respectable. I am not prepared to predict when this moment might next occur, but perhaps discussions like this one will help hasten it.

People had better start to find their voice for the emerging debate. Finance will be reregulated, I am sure, and who gets to design the new controls matters enormously. If manufacturing executives are not at the table, for instance, they should not expect that the new system will be designed to foster the rebirth of American manufacturing. If housing advocates are not engaged in the debate, new policies will not address the housing crisis. Likewise for labor, small business, and borrowers of every kind. If citizens do not stand up for their own self-interest, then others will determine it for them. The subject of money, in other words, is too important to be left to bankers.

Anytime, any place, in the air and on the ground, Federal Express
is working to meet the needs of business throughout the world.

Additional Copies

To order additional copies of *The Trouble With Money* for friends or colleagues, please write to The Larger Agenda Series, Whittle Direct Books, 505 Market St., Knoxville, TN 37902. Please include the recipient's name, mailing address, and, where applicable, title, company name, and type of business.

For a single copy, please enclose a check for $11.95 payable to The Larger Agenda Series. When ordering 10 or more books, enclose $9.95 for each; for orders of 50 or more books, enclose $7.95 for each. If you wish to place an order by phone, call 1-800-284-1956.

Please allow six weeks for delivery.
Tennessee residents must add 7¾ percent sales tax.